WINNING CORPORATE REPUTATION STRATEGIES

WINNING CORPORATE REPUTATION STRATEGIES

Lessons from Asia Pacific

edited by

Mark Chong and Jin Montesano

Singapore • Boston • Burr Ridge, IL • Dubuque, IA • Madison, WI • New York • San Francisco
St. Louis • Bangkok • Kuala Lumpur • Lisbon • London • Madrid • Mexico City
Milan • Montreal • New Delhi • Seoul • Sydney • Taipei • Toronto

The McGraw-Hill Companies

McGraw-Hill Professional

WINNING CORPORATE REPUTATION STRATEGIES
Lessons from Asia Pacific

10 9 8 7 6 5 4 3 2 1
CTP SLP
20 13 12

When ordering this title, use **ISBN 978-007-132703-9** or **MHID 007-132703-7**

Printed in Singapore

All proceeds from the sale of this book will be donated to
Make-A-Wish Foundation

CONTENTS

FOREWORD

When I was invited to contribute the Foreword to this book, I wholeheartedly agreed for a number of reasons. Why? Because in today's complex business environment, *reputation matters*. The difference between a good and a great company is the value and trust placed by its stakeholders in that company's reputation. Good reputation helps recruit the best talent in the market, retain the top talent you already have, win business partners more effectively, and maximize your influence with other key stakeholders essential for your business to operate and win every day. If you do not believe these statements, then this book is not for you, because that is the first belief you must have in order to maximize the value of a good Corporate Affairs team. First, I have great appreciation for Corporate Affairs professionals today. They are tasked with managing a 24/7 cycle of news, opinions, and issues that cut across a range of decision makers and influencers—from regulators, politicians, and special interest groups to investors, business partners, and consumers. Often, they do their jobs with the leanest number of people on their teams and with the smallest budgets. Their work cuts across a wide swath of disciplines: from partnering with HR to step up employee engagement through internal communications, managing CSR initiatives, and working with the media—and increasingly, social media—to address questions and concerns about the company, to negotiating with governments to reconsider a regulation or policy that is bad for business.

As a global business executive, I have had the privilege of managing and leading senior teams in large organizations for over 30 years—operating in the United States and Japan as well as across Asia and the Pacific. Most of my leadership experience has been with General Electric (GE), but I started my career with a large Japanese trading firm leading M&A transactions across multiple industries and sectors. Throughout my career, and especially in my general management and leadership roles, I have managed cross-functional teams that always include a company's key functional roles such as HR, Finance, Operations, Risk, and Legal. Over the years, however, I have observed the rise of Corporate Affairs professionals moving steadily to senior positions on management teams. Today, at GE, these professionals have a firm seat at the table and play an important role in bringing the outside world into GE, and helping us engage in a dialogue with our external stakeholders about GE. Obviously, this is not a phenomenon taking place in my company alone; many of my corporate peers running global corporations have increasingly come to rely on sound, in-house "reputation counsels" for advice on steering their corporate ships through what has become a highly complex and interconnected world of stakeholders and issues.

Which brings me to the second reason why I agreed to write this Foreword. As one of my former Corporate Affairs advisors once told me, "The notion of public relations, to the extent that there is a 'public' to relate with, is essentially dead. We must consider corporate reputation today from the lens of the stakeholder, and address stakeholders' specific concerns."

Because of this insight, I appreciated the editors' decision to organize the book's chapters by stakeholder group, featuring a case study of a company managing a business issue by addressing a particular stakeholder's issues and concerns as part of its navigation toward a positive business outcome. Stakeholders, simply put, are individuals or groups that have some kind of "stake" in your business. Sometimes, these stakeholders can determine whether your business will remain viable, such as a regulatory agency responsible for licensing your operation or a government ministry that decides to restrict how, where, and when a company may offer its products and services. Other stakeholders, such as the media, are both a stakeholder and a critical influencer of other stakeholders.

The most important reason for contributing this Foreword, however, is simply because I am pleased to be part of a unique publication that focuses on Corporate Affairs strategies with specific challenges and opportunities found in Asia Pacific. Home to the world's fastest-growing economies and absolute juggernauts such as India, China, and Indonesia, Asia Pacific is often cited as the future of growth and expansion—not only for the Fortune 500 companies, but also for homegrown Asian companies with regional and global aspirations. But as many of my peers will attest, the complexities of operating in the developing, or emerging, markets cannot be underestimated, especially in the area of reputation risks—and opportunities—for business. These chapters offer a dense snapshot of the diversity of issues and challenges faced by many global companies, such as Diageo, Monsanto, and Kraft Foods. For executives who have wondered about the role of Corporate Affairs in business, these pages will offer you a stronger understanding of this function's value, expertise, and potential to contribute to a business leader's objectives. A newly minted General Manager or an experienced CEO running a business in Asia will gain new insight and understanding of the role Corporate Affairs can—and should—play as a critical partner to business.

Yoshiaki Fujimori
President and CEO
JS Group Corporation

PREFACE

This book is the result of several conversations we had with each other over many months. We noticed that there were a number of books on public relations aimed at PR practitioners, but there were fewer books on corporate reputation management—and virtually none on corporate reputation management in Asia Pacific that were aimed at the C-suite.

In our respective teaching and professional roles, we also found ourselves lamenting the absence of a book that could show graduate students and senior Corporate Public Affairs executives what "good" looks like in Asia Pacific. So, we put our heads together—along with several eminent colleagues in the region—to attempt to fill this gap.

This book contains seven case studies that show how several companies addressed the reputational challenges they faced in Asia Pacific. In addition, two special chapters shed light on the unique Corporate Public Affairs landscape in Asia Pacific's two most important economies—China and India.

We wrote this book primarily for the chief executive who is new to Asia Pacific; for this person, the book could serve as a primer on strategies to protect the firm's license to operate and ensure its sustainability. This book is also suitable for the senior Corporate Public Affairs executive or executive MBA student who is interested in gleaning lessons learnt by other companies in the region.

We hope the reputation strategies captured in this book will give readers a jump start in understanding and successfully navigating a complex, rapidly evolving environment.

We would like to express our heartfelt thanks to Yoshiaki Fujimori, all of our contributors, and our reviewers for helping us to make this book a reality.

Mark Chong, Jin Montesano
Singapore
December 2011

CONTRIBUTORS

WAYNE BURNS is Director of the Centre for Corporate Public Affairs (operates internationally) and a Director of the Asia Pacific economics and public policy firm Allen Consulting Group. He writes, consults, and teaches executive education internationally on best-practice stakeholder engagement, issues management, and corporate responsibility. Wayne consults on public affairs management across Asia and has 25 years' experience in business, political advisory, journalism, and public affairs. He has a BA in Communication Journalism from Charles Sturt University in Australia and a postgraduate qualification in community involvement from Boston College in the United States. ■

FEI CHE joined Kraft Foods China in July 2009 as Director, Corporate Affairs. In this role, she is responsible for Kraft Foods' Government Affairs, Corporate Communications, and Community Affairs in China. Fei is a seasoned corporate communications and public affairs professional. Prior to joining Kraft Foods China, she was Vice President, Corporate & Government Affairs, for AB Inbev. In this role, she set up the Corporate Affairs functions in China and Korea and managed the company's Corporate Affairs activities across Asia.

From 2004 to 2006, Fei worked as Director, Corporate Communication and Community Affairs, for Honeywell Greater China Region. She led the corporate reputation building for Honeywell in China and launched an award-winning community project focusing on children's safety at home and in schools. From 1999 to 2002, Fei worked as Director, Public Affairs and Corporate Communications, for Bristol-Myers Squibb (BMS) China. In this role, she built BMS's corporate reputation and led consumer and patient education campaigns. She launched hepatitis B prevention programs for rural Chinese children in partnership with the

Ministry of Health's Center for Disease Control. Prior to BMS, Fei was the Chief Legal Representative of Weber Shandwick Worldwide Public Relations in Beijing.

Fei began her career as a journalist for CCTV in 1987. Later, she worked as a producer and anchorwoman for Asia Business News (today's CNBC Asia), Dow Jones' Asia Satellite TV Broadcast. Fei graduated from Columbia University in New York with a master's degree in Science from the School of Journalism (1991) and a master's degree in International Affairs from the School of International Affairs and Public Administration (1992). She graduated from Peking University in 1980 with a bachelor's degree in English and a master's degree in American Literature. ■

MARK CHONG, **PhD**, is Associate Professor of Corporate Communication Practice at Singapore Management University (SMU), where he teaches in the undergraduate and Executive Master in Communication Management programs. He is also a member of the SMU Case Writing Editorial Board. Prior to academia, Mark worked as a corporate and marketing communication professional in Asia. Mark received his PhD from Cornell University. This is his third book. ■

HARVEY GLICK, **PhD**, is Senior Director, Asia Regulatory Policy and Scientific Affairs, at Monsanto. He has been actively involved in agricultural research and development for over 35 years. He studied agronomy at McGill University in Montreal, where he received a Bachelor of Science in Agriculture. He obtained his master's degree in Plant Physiology at the University of Manitoba and received his PhD in Plant Physiology and Biology at the University of Manitoba on a full scholarship. He has also completed an executive business management program at the University of Western Ontario.

After completing his formal education, he joined the Canadian Wheat Board, an organization involved in international grain marketing. In 1985, after three years with the Wheat Board, he joined Monsanto as it was beginning to develop crop biotechnology programs.

Over the past 25 years at Monsanto, Harvey has lived and worked in Canada, Belgium, and the United States and is currently based in Singapore. He has held various positions in the technology, commercial development, and marketing departments. He has visited and worked in agricultural production systems in many different regions of the world with the objective of bringing new agricultural technology to producers. He helped introduce the first biotech crop to Canadian farmers in 1995 and has been actively involved in the development of biotech crops for Europe, Asia, and the Americas. Currently, he is Senior Director, Asia, for Regulatory Policy and Scientific Affairs and is directly involved in bringing the next generation of plant biotechnology products to farmers in Asia. He is a frequent speaker at conferences focused on agricultural biotechnology and sustainable food production systems. He serves on the board of directors for the International Life Sciences Institute Southeast Asia Region and the Asia Food Information Council. ■

JIN MONTESANO is Vice President, Corporate and Government Affairs Asia Pacific, at Kraft Foods. She is a public affairs practitioner with over 17 years of experience in advocacy, communications, and government relations, having worked across government, NPOs, and the corporate sector. She joined Kraft Foods in March 2009 as Vice President of Corporate and Government Affairs, Asia Pacific. She leads the company's regional corporate reputation building program, including CSR, corporate PR, government relations, and issues and crisis management. Prior to her current role, Jin served four years with GE Capital, where she established and led the region's strategic communications and public affairs strategy for GE's consumer finance operations in Asia, GE Money, as Vice President of Communications.

She joined GE after serving as Director of Corporate and Government Affairs for GlaxoSmithKline's Asia Pacific operations based in Singapore from 2000 to 2005. A public affairs specialist, she started her career in Washington influencing US–Korea economic and trade policy issues on Capitol Hill as the Congressional Affairs Director for the Korea Economic Institute. She also served as an analyst for the US Defense Department. She began her corporate career with Ogilvy and Mather Public Relations after moving to Asia in 1999.

Jin received a Bachelor of Arts in English Literature from Columbia College of Columbia University in New York, and a Master of Public Affairs from Princeton University's Woodrow Wilson School of Public and International Affairs. She is also a published author on international political and economic topics concerning Asia. ■

BASSKARAN NAIR is Senior Vice President, Group Corporate Marketing and Communications, at CapitaLand Limited and an Adjunct Associate Professor at the Lee Kuan Yew School of Public Policy, National University of Singapore. He was previously an Equity Partner and CEO of an international communications firm.

Basskaran has been a board member of Certis CISCO Security, a Temasek-linked company, since July 2005. In January 2011, he also became a board member of the Media Development Authority. In November 2010, Basskaran was conferred the Public Service Medal by the President of the Republic of Singapore for distinguished service to the nation. In 1997, the Institute of Public Relations of Singapore (IPRS) nominated him Fellow of IPRS, and subsequently recognized him as the "PR Professional of the Year 2004." In 2008, he was awarded the IPRS "Lifetime Achievement Award." He has authored several books, the latest of which is *From Main Street to Cyber Street: Changes in the Practice of Communication*, focusing on the role of new media in public communications. ■

JEFF RICHARDSON is co-founder and CEO of the social media agency The Online Circle, based in Melbourne, Australia. He entered the online marketing industry over 15 years ago, when the Internet began to boom and Internet marketing was a largely uncharted field. With a background in corporate marketing and an understanding of business needs, Jeff sees social media through mature eyes, recognizing not just the opportunities but also the risks. ■

OPHIRA SAMUEL–BHATIA has been in the public relations business in India for 15 years and has consulted and worked with a range of both Indian and multinational clients. Ophira began her career in 1996 with a local public relations firm, at a time when Indian businesses were experiencing the first rush of success with the new liberalization of the economy. She has wide-ranging expertise across key industries and sectors, including infrastructure, information technology, food, media and entertainment, financial services, government, and trade promotion. Ophira has been involved in work around corporate reputation management and planning, crisis management, corporate positioning, communication skills training, product launches, branding, market entry, financial communications, social engagement programs, and employee strategies. In her current role, Ophira is Director, Corporate Affairs South Asia and Indochina for Kraft Foods and is responsible for the company's corporate reputation program, internal communications, CSR, corporate public relations, government relations and issues, and crisis management. Prior to joining Kraft Foods, Ophira led the Mumbai office of Edelman India—the world's largest independent public relations firm—and worked closely to promote firms' agendas in the evolving space that is PR in India. ■

SIMON YOUNG is Director of Regulatory Affairs, Unilever Global Home and Personal Care. He is a microbiologist by training, with over 25 years' experience in pharmaceutical quality assurance, and pharmaceutical and consumer product regulatory and external affairs. He was based in Bangkok and Shanghai between 2003 and 2011, with regulatory affairs responsibility for the Unilever home and personal care business in Asia, and is now based in the United Kingdom with Unilever covering global home and personal care regulatory affairs.

Before joining Unilever, Simon was responsible for pharmaceutical regulatory affairs for Glaxo pharmaceuticals, covering Asia Pacific and Latin America. Prior to this, he had a career in pharmaceutical quality management based in the United Kingdom, the United States, and Saudi Arabia.

He was extensively involved in the ASEAN cosmetic regulatory process from 1998, acting as a consultant to various regulatory bodies and industry associations in ASEAN. He also served on behalf of Thailand and the ASEAN Cosmetic Association as secretary to the ASEAN Cosmetic Scientific Body from its inception in 2004 until he left the region in 2011. He is a frequent speaker at regulatory affairs conferences across Asia and an active member of Asian and European industry associations. ■

I would like to dedicate this book to my parents.

— *Mark Chong*

This book is dedicated to my dear husband, Michael, for his support, patience, and loyalty. I also dedicate it to Pradeep Pant and Nancy Daigler, two of the most authentic and inspiring leaders I have ever had the privilege to work with and to learn from.

— *Jin Montesano*

1

CHAPTER

Introduction

Jin Montesano

STRATEGIC CORPORATE PUBLIC AFFAIRS IN ASIA: IS THE PROBLEM SUPPLY OR DEMAND?

In early 2011, faculty members from Singapore Management University invited a select group of senior executives to discuss the university's ambitious plans for a new degree program in Communications Management. Both Mark Chong and I were present for this discussion, he as a member of faculty and I as a member of the program's advisory panel. The discussion began with a fact that surprised many: according to a survey conducted in Asia, the compensation packages for Corporate Public Affairs practitioners in the region took giant leaps at every step up the career ladder, with the jump in compensation between "Manager" and "Executive" amounting to as much as 51 per cent to 78 per cent. Surveying the Tokyo, Hong Kong, and Singapore markets—the key "hubs" for Corporate Public Affairs talent in the region—a leading headhunting firm, Hudson (2011), concluded that this financial bounty was not as pronounced as with other functions or geographic regions. Indeed, a persistent and significant "talent gap" seemed to exist in the supply of seasoned practitioners who were able to think first as business leaders, then as functional experts, in the area of reputation and stakeholder management.

As the group discussed ways to tackle this "supply" problem, my mind was set firmly on "demand." Having worked in in-house roles for three global companies in Asia over the last 12 years, each role being larger and more complex than the last, I knew that the supply problem was real: in each of these roles, including my current one at Kraft Foods, about 50 per cent of my time is focused on recruitment, talent development, and capability building. Yet I was of the view that the real driver of these rising pay scales was not the supply problem: it was the exponential growth in the number of companies in the region that were beginning to understand the need for and aggressively invest in the best "reputation chiefs" that money could buy.

AS THE COMPETITIVE LANDSCAPE SHIFTS, SO TOO DOES THE FUNCTION'S ROLE IN ASIA

While most business executives understand the role of more traditional functions such as Sales, Finance, and Marketing better than they do the role of Corporate Public Affairs, there has been a significant shift in executive thinking in the last decade regarding the value that this function can play in delivering business outcomes in Asia. In the course of this shift, the function has grown from a primarily tactical focus and a stress on issues and crisis management to the embrace of a more strategic role in the business. In high-performing companies, Corporate Public Affairs professionals have become indispensable business partners, executing against longer-term stakeholder management plans with measurable performance benchmarks. According to a 2009 study conducted by the Centre for Corporate Public Affairs, 65 per cent of senior Public Affairs executives in the Asia Pacific region were members of the senior management team, and 70 per cent of survey respondents had a direct reporting relationship to the CEO, regional managing director, or regional president.

Asia has taken center stage as a critical region for the rapid future growth of the world's global corporations. It is prominent on the agenda of every global board. With over 30 markets, 2,000 languages, and over 60 per cent of the world's population residing in this part of the world (Wikipedia, 2011), the social, political, cultural, and economic complexities of the region pose immense challenges to companies unfamiliar with the sheer diversity of its marketplaces.

In the meantime, competition is no longer limited to a fight for market share among US, European, and Australian firms. Homegrown companies are quickly conquering domestic markets across Asia. In their quest for growth and expansion, they are moving aggressively to build regional and even global footprints. With one eye cast on "making the quarter number," many astute

CEOs and General Managers in the region have the other eye squarely on the longer-term game plan. They seek to ensure a favorable—or at least more predictable—business climate even as they operate in the most dynamic societies and economies in the world. As Asia becomes more financially material to the total revenue growth of global corporations, business leaders are under ever greater pressure to deliver business performance. Failing to navigate the policy, regulatory, and political complexities of Asian business environments can have a clear and significant negative impact on a growing number of global corporations. Successful leaders who operate in the region today therefore require Corporate Public Affairs teams equipped to support the business vision and to go beyond being the "issues and crisis people" or "spin team."

Whether you are a General Manager heading up a business in the region, an experienced CEO arriving in Asia to lead an organization, or a business leader about to embark on a major initiative with implications for a broad group of stakeholders (such as a restructuring or M&A), this book is written for you. For other executives interested in knowing how all the various disciplines under the Corporate Public Affairs banner "come together" to deliver against key business objectives, in better understanding what "good" looks like in this field, and in mastering practical approaches to challenges in your own business, this book is also for you.

A UNIQUE APPROACH TO UNDERSTAND STAKEHOLDER MANAGEMENT IN ASIA

Winning Corporate Reputation Strategies: Lessons from Asia Pacific may not be the first book to delve into Corporate Public Affairs strategies that have played a key role in delivering business outcomes, but we believe that it is the first to look at corporate reputation issues from an Asian regional perspective. Each chapter offers a case study of a specific business challenge that a company has faced while operating in Asia and of the strategies used to achieve successful business outcomes. Each case study is written by a senior practitioner or academic living and working in Asia.

The first three chapters explore significant challenges faced by three companies—China Light & Power, Diageo, and Monsanto—whose "licenses to operate" are under threat as a result of shifting dynamics in the socio-political environment. These chapters detail the companies' respective approaches to managing these changing landscapes.

The next three chapters offer a closer look at one company—or in one case a group of companies, through an industry association—achieving business objectives by leveraging targeted strategies addressing specific stakeholder concerns. We also include a special chapter on the rapid rise of social media in Asia Pacific and its impact not just on global brands, but increasingly on corporate reputations.

The book's final two chapters zero in on the challenges and opportunities for corporate reputation management in two of the most complex markets in the world, and certainly in Asia—India and China. These two globally critical markets are defined by the Asia Pacific region's most constantly shape-shifting socio-political and economic environments. No book on corporate reputation in Asia would be complete without addressing the two countries that will set regional and global agendas for many years to come.

CHAPTER TWO

This chapter is a case study about a 100-year-old company, China Light & Power Holdings (CLP). It is a US$7-billion energy conglomerate that faced a reputation crisis because of its perceived contribution to Hong Kong's infamously poor air quality.

When a local environmental NGO began to influence public policy and community behavior to reduce air pollution in Hong Kong, CLP became a lightning rod for the city's air pollution problems. Senior management at CLP decided to tackle this issue head on, taking key decisions about how the company would operate, such as reducing its carbon footprint in Hong Kong. CLP also decided to engage with its stakeholders—namely, its customers—whose behaviors would have an impact on energy demand and sustainable energy use.

Sending a clear message to its stakeholders that CLP could not sustain its business in Hong Kong unless the city itself remained a sustainable place to live and work, CLP effectively began a dialogue to co-create a future that would see improved air quality and sustainable energy usage in Hong Kong.

CHAPTER THREE

In this chapter, we review the case study of Diageo's business in Asia Pacific. Diageo is the world's leading premium drinks business, with well-known brands such as Johnnie Walker, Smirnoff, and Baileys. Its "license to operate" was threatened by excessive drinking among youths and alcohol misuse. This led to calls for urgent regulation and societal responses to irresponsible alcohol consumption.

Diageo tackled the issue by focusing on the three areas in which it could make the most impact: setting high standards for self-regulation in responsible marketing, implementing initiatives to raise awareness and change behavior to minimize alcohol abuse, and promoting effective and targeted alcohol policies through a balanced debate with legislators and policy makers at the global, regional, and country levels.

CHAPTER FOUR

Here we discuss the challenges faced by companies that are unable to conduct an effective dialogue with customers because of a growing cacophony of other stakeholder voices that are communicating with those customers—leaving the customers confused and unable to make clear business decisions. In the case of Monsanto, the customer is the farmer.

Asia Pacific is home to 60 per cent of the world's population and nearly 80 per cent of the world's farmers; yet these farmers are among the most resource-poor farmers in the world, with low incomes and little formal education. As a leading biotechnology company, Monsanto makes it a critical business priority to help farmers understand the role technology can play in protecting crops and improving productivity.

As farmers in Asia were bombarded by messages with a range of opinions—from government, NGOs, community leaders, consumers, and media—Monsanto began a concerted effort to engage these opinion leaders and decision makers on topics of concern regarding agriculture, science, and biotechnology. Its approach was to drive a more science-based discussion about biotechnology and focus on the role biotechnology plays in achieving sustainable agriculture—something all stakeholders see as an important end-goal of farming.

CHAPTER FIVE

We offer an example of the kinds of regulatory and policy success that come from a collaborative partnership between government and industry. With the cooperation of regulators, the ASEAN Secretariat, and industry, the ASEAN Economic Ministers agreed to harmonize policies and standards for the cosmetics industry that would increase consumer confidence in product safety and reduce technical barriers to trade.

A number of important lessons are shared from this chapter when working with government, including the clear ownership of the issue from within the political leadership and a clear "win-win-win" strategy for consumers, industry, and regulators.

CHAPTER SIX

This chapter examines the considerations, approaches, and outcomes of a strategic community program initiated by Kraft Foods in China, in partnership with the China Youth Development Foundation. The chapter outlines the local management team's business rationale for investing in such a program and the lessons learned.

The authors assert that the establishment of a strategic community platform that is scalable, sustainable, and socially relevant reinforces Kraft Foods' core business strategies in China, namely, to strengthen relationships with key business partners, to increase employee engagement through employee volunteerism, and to strengthen the company's corporate reputation and profile in China.

CHAPTER SEVEN

This chapter delves into one part of Singapore Airlines' operations, and how the world-famous "SQ" brand is able to realize its brand promise and experience through a strategic internal communications and employee engagement program focused on strong corporate values, training, and communication that extends from pilots and cabin crew to the ground staff in the organization.

We demonstrate that SIA's internal communications program is not only comprehensive, ongoing, and intensive, but also unique in that content, frequency, and channels of communication are highly targeted to specific employee groups within the company that need specifically tailored communication, such as the Cabin Crew division. More important, linking the company's core values to employee performance and reiterating what it means to "live these values" has been a critical factor in SIA's success at building one of the strongest corporate brands in the world, from the inside out.

CHAPTER EIGHT

We look at a new area of reputation management that many companies are still grappling with: the rise of social media and its impact on business and reputation. Jeff Richardson examines the various roles that social media can play in managing a company's reputation.

Looking at five different companies and their specific reputation challenges, the author examines the role social media played in each of these situations and the valuable lessons learned. Richardson argues that there are essentially five roles that companies need to think about when it comes to social media:

1. Determine the reality;
2. Manage the impact of public commentary;
3. Manage service providers and/or staff who know just enough to be dangerous;
4. Identify intentional subterfuge, misrepresentation of facts, and fraudulent competitive activity designed to harm your brand; and
5. Manage staff, including education, training, and monitoring.

CHAPTER NINE

Ophira Samuel-Bhatia shares her views about the changes, challenges, and opportunities for building reputation and business success in India. With a growing middle class and increasing affluence, India is one of the world's most powerful and attractive consumer markets. At the same time, it has low levels of literacy, poor access to affordable health care, poor infrastructure, and 400 million citizens living below the poverty line.

Samuel-Bhatia advises that companies must keep these paradoxes and sensitivities in mind when operating in India. She also talks about the key imperatives companies should adopt when building reputation and communications programs.

India has seen a rise in judicial activism and calls for greater scrutiny of ethical practices, an explosion of digital media and citizen journalism, and rising demands of corporate competitiveness. These elements create opportunities for India's

Corporate Affairs professionals to play a role in building strong reputations for corporations and strengthening the public's trust in these companies.

CHAPTER TEN

Basskaran Nair of CapitaLand shares his views about effective Corporate Public Affairs strategies in the context of the socio-political landscape in China. He reviews major events that have shaped the reputation and brand image of China on the world stage, and the implications China's self-image has on thinking about corporate reputation building.

The field of Corporate Public Affairs is at a relatively early stage of development in China, even among global companies present in the country. Understanding the rise of China in the context of how it perceives itself and wants to be perceived by others should be a critical part of how any Corporate Public Affairs strategy is considered or executed in China. Foreign companies with a long-term growth strategy in China are advised to invest in programs that invest in the community and on priority issues of the Chinese government.

THE BOTTOM LINE

While each case study in this book offers a wealth of insights and lessons for successful stakeholder strategies, several recurrent themes merit highlighting here.

■ A Single-stakeholder Problem Often Requires a Multiple-stakeholder Solution

Effective Public Affairs strategies require multiple-stakeholder advocacy and engagement, pushing and pulling the right program levers, initiatives, and partnerships at the right time and through the right channels.

For instance, Monsanto's challenge with improving its communication with farmers was a real business issue, but tackling the issue required engagement and dialogue with a much broader range of stakeholders in a coordinated and specific way.

One Size Does Not Fit All

Understand all of your key stakeholders' concerns and opinions and how they interact with and influence one another. Strategic engagement requires a tailored plan to address each stakeholder group's specific concerns.

SIA's tailored approach to each employee stakeholder group is a great example of this approach in action. While many companies would see "employees" as a single stakeholder, SIA went a step beyond that view. It broke this stakeholder group down into even more specific groups and developed programs to address each of those groups effectively.

A "License to Operate" is Earned, Not Granted

With globalization, a 24/7 news cycle, and "citizen journalism" thanks to Web 2.0, a company's reputation and its "license to operate" can be revoked in a matter of minutes, not days or months.

The Diageo and CPL case studies each underscore the reality that doing business in Asia is not a right, but rather a privilege earned every day by demonstrating—through self-regulation, responsible leadership, and stakeholder engagement platforms—that co-creating the future through win-win solutions for society and business is a way to protect a company's operating environment and retain its "license to operate."

This last point frames the lessons of each of the following chapters. A Corporate Public Affairs team can best be leveraged by an organization when the team is led by a professional with a seat at the strategic table. When the function is not represented at the management or leadership level at which strategic business issues are discussed and decided, it is often relegated to reactive, *ad hoc* activities such as internal communications, media relations, or issues and crisis management. With a Corporate Public Affairs team unable to contribute at the strategic level, an organization is destined to under-leverage what many business leaders regard as the function's most useful role.

Corporate Public Affairs delivers most when it serves as the strategic window through which a business understands the nuances, trends, and constantly changing dynamics of the external business environment. The function should, in turn, inform strategies to mitigate risk, strengthen reputation, and drive stakeholder engagement platforms that deliver business objectives. Rather than a back-end support role, a high-performing Corporate Public Affairs team takes on a front-end strategic approach by operating at the coalface of business-critical issues and strategically and proactively manages the company's reputation and its stakeholders.

Corporate Public Affairs is a fascinating and challenging frontier in a modern corporation, especially in the emerging markets. For companies entering into previously unknown and highly complex markets such as Indonesia, China, or India, investment in an effective Corporate Public Affairs function is critical to delivering long-term business outcomes. As diverse societal stakeholders take on more prominent roles in determining the viability or success of business strategies in Asia, Corporate Public Affairs is increasingly viewed as a "must have" function for firms with aggressive growth agendas in this dynamic socio-political environment.

References

The Hudson Report—Asia. Retrieved from http://sg.hudson.com/documents/Hudson_Report_Q3_2011_Asia.pdf.

Wikipedia. Asia. Retrieved from http://en.wikipedia.org/wiki/Asia.

2

CHAPTER

Pollution and the Fragrant Harbor—Why China Light & Power's Stakeholder Engagement with Customers May Help Clear the Air in Hong Kong

WAYNE BURNS

Executive Summary

First and foremost, a company's relationship with its customers is simple: the company seeks to delight its customers, and the customers buy the company's goods or services. But not always. Customers can also be among a corporation's most important stakeholders in issues beyond the traditional customer relationship, which can affect the future of the company.

For China Light & Power Holdings (CLP), an annual US$7–billion energy generation and distribution conglomerate operating across Asia Pacific, public health, environmental sustainability, quality of life issues, and business concerns about air pollution in Hong Kong prompted it to forge a new relationship with its customers. The customers are now CLP's stakeholders in reducing air pollution and mitigating business risk in the company's home market.

BACKGROUND

Following more than 100 years in business, China Light & Power Holdings (CLP)—a publicly listed Asia Pacific energy generator (US$7 billion annual revenues)—is determined to be a profitable enterprise for at least another century or two. Headquartered in Hong Kong—and with 50 energy generation and distribution assets in Australia, China, Hong Kong, India, Taiwan, Thailand, and Vietnam—CLP has determined that if it wants to continue to expand its business, it needs to make sure it has the support of investors, regulators, lawmakers, and others who have a stake in its business—including its customers in its home base. Hong Kong has been struggling with serious air quality and air pollution for about two decades. Air pollution is a constant issue for discussion and discourse in Hong Kong—in the media, in shops and restaurants, on trains and buses, in hospitals and medical clinics, in the Legislature, and in the offices and boardrooms of local and multinational corporations and their peak business chambers.

The blame for Hong Kong's poor air quality is often slated home to CLP, which is one of the two Hong Kong electricity generators and distributors, and the larger. The not-for-profit environment lobby group Clear The Air, which was established solely to influence public policy and community behavior to reduce air pollution in Hong Kong, says power plants account for 70 per cent of the city's total greenhouse gas emissions, and that CLP is responsible for more than half of these.

There is still considerable debate about the causes of Hong Kong's air quality, which on some days is so poor that schools close and special health warnings are issued for residents with respiratory or heart conditions to stay indoors. There is little doubt that Hong Kong's air quality is affected regularly by pollution from intensive manufacturing and commercial activity in China's Pearl River Delta, which includes Guangdong Province, bordering Hong Kong. And Hong Kong has the highest road traffic density in the world. Motor vehicles are the second-largest source of greenhouse gas emissions in the traffic-congested city.

But while these factors are real and important, the city's legislators, regulators, and activist interest groups see CLP as a big part of the problem. And so do many of CLP's customers. Sensing rightly that CLP's greenhouse gas emissions and their impact on the community were looming as an issue that affected the attitudes and behaviors of customers, activist interest groups, legislators, and regulators in Hong Kong and in other markets where it operates, the corporation's senior management team, led by its CEO, decided to confront the issue.

The management team decided that it would work with a broad range of stakeholders in its home market of Hong Kong (and in its other markets) to reduce the company's overall greenhouse gas emissions from power generation. While this appeared good business in existing markets and would assist CLP to sustain and expand its operations in those markets, it was also recognized that reducing its own emissions may assist the company's future entry into new markets.

CLP's plan, however, was not only to take active steps to reduce its carbon footprint in Hong Kong (it invested US$1.15 billion to upgrade its main coal-fired Castle Peak power station in the city). It decided to also engage its stakeholders—individuals, groups, and institutions with an interest in its business and its impact on the community—whose advocacy, behaviors, and energy use had a direct impact on energy demand and sustainable energy use.

At the front and center of the company's stakeholder landscape were its customers. CLP has two million customers in Hong Kong, including about 200,000 small and medium enterprises. CLP's thinking was that if it could engage its customers in its efforts to reduce greenhouse gas emissions in Hong Kong, its commitment and task would also be "owned" by many of its customers and other stakeholders. According to senior CLP executives, this was not only "the right thing to do," but also a powerful message from the company that it recognized that it could not sustain its business in Hong Kong unless the city itself remained a sustainable place to live and do business.

As well as "the right thing to do," CLP's decision can be seen also as good business sense. Providing sustained returns to shareholders (core to CLP's business strategy) can only continue if the company is given the "social license" (or community permission) to continue to do business.

STAKEHOLDER LANDSCAPE

As one of two energy generators in Hong Kong, CLP operates two power stations there: Castle Peak, one of the world's largest coal-fired power stations, in the New Territories of Hong Kong (on the border with Mainland China); and Black Point, one of the world's largest gas-generated power stations in Hong Kong. The company also maintains the Penny's Bay backup power station powered by oil distillate. It can be up and running in nine minutes in case either of its two primary generation plants goes offline. CLP also has power-generating interests in the neighboring Chinese province of Guangdong: a nuclear power plant (from which it purchases electricity for use in Hong Kong); and a hydroelectricity pumped storage plant, also in Guangdong.

Despite—or possibly because of—Hong Kong's air quality problems, residents of the city (whose name in Cantonese means "fragrant harbor") have been very vocal about air pollution in their city, where it is estimated that visibility is less than eight kilometers for 30 per cent of the year. Local media outlets focus on this issue continually.

The Hong Kong government's Air Pollution Index, which was established in 1995 and issues daily air quality reports and warnings, continues to be controversial because of claims it does not capture all the harmful elements when assessing air quality. Greenpeace launched its own "Real Pollution Index" measurement in 2008 to present what it claims are more accurate data. Media outlets in Hong Kong have reported World Health Organization standards are ten per cent to 64 per cent more stringent than the government's existing index. Following political and public pressure, the Hong Kong government agreed to establish new air quality measures by the end of 2011.

A local nongovernmental organization (NGO), Clear The Air, was established in 1997 to specifically pressure the government, regulators, and Hong Kong's two power generators—including CLP—to address and reduce air pollution. It also manages an on-going campaign to reduce motor vehicle engine idling in congested traffic (it is estimated that Hong Kong's congested traffic environment contributes up to a third of all air pollution in the city). Clear The Air has only 1,500 members. However, it is very vocal and well networked with environmental, health, and city planning activists, and business groups.

The organized stakeholder groups that contribute to public debate and private lobbying about Hong Kong's air pollution include medical organizations and public health advocates. They have claimed that roadside pollution alone contributes to almost 3,000 premature deaths a year and 90,000 hospital admissions. Business groups, including the Hong Kong Chamber of Commerce and specialist industry associations, have voiced their concerns, arguing that air pollution is having a negative effect on Hong Kong's reputation as one of Asia's financial and business hubs. Some have complained that Hong Kong's air pollution is making Singapore (in particular) a more desirable center for corporate regional headquarters.

Anyone living in Hong Kong, or a regular visitor there, has an opinion about air pollution in the city, and it is most likely to be a strong opinion. If the individual is a resident, he will most likely see that emissions from power generation are a big part of the air quality problem. And as well as having a "stake" in the issue as a citizen, there is a good chance that the resident will also be a CLP customer or shareholder.

STRATEGIES CONSIDERED

Power generating and distribution companies are by their nature primarily left-brained organizations—that is, focused on addressing technical challenges, and understanding and tackling complex engineering conundrums based on data. In these organizations, the CEO also needs to make sense of the socio-political or "right brain" landscape—assisted and supported often by central management functions, including Corporate Public Affairs, Human Resources, and Marketing. This is the realm of public policy, politics, stakeholders, the media, NGOs, and public discourse and debate.

CLP has a considered and documented approach to stakeholder engagement, which it published in its 2010 progress report on its Energy Vision emission reduction targets. That approach includes balancing the social, environmental, and economic interests of stakeholders when making business decisions. The company's approach to stakeholders is entrenched in its business model, because in its markets and lines of business, the socio-political "license to operate" is so important to its being able to operate profitably and to make long-term investment decisions.

As the CLP leadership team considered its approach to "do something" about air quality in Hong Kong, it wanted to develop and execute a strategy that addressed business issues in its hometown, but with an eye also on how strategy and execution may resonate in its other markets. To develop its strategy and plan to execute it, CLP examined what contributed to Hong Kong's air pollution:

1. CLP's own emissions, and that of the Hong Kong Electric Company (which operates a coal-fired power station in the city);
2. Emissions from massive economic activity in the Pearl River Delta area in China;
3. Emissions from motor vehicles in the city; and
4. Emissions from economic activity in Hong Kong.

The company examined what it could do from the supply side. Logic dictated it could address emissions from its plants in Hong Kong. It sets targets out to 2025 to reduce its emissions and, as noted earlier in this chapter, conducted a US$1.15 billion refit of its Castle Peak coal-fired power station. However, as it examined what contributed to air pollution in Hong Kong, CLP's senior management, with counsel and support from its Group Public Affairs and Marketing and Customer Service management functions, decided to address the "demand" side too. And this included customers as key stakeholders.

The following table illustrates CLP's approach to extend its efforts to reduce emissions beyond its own direct impact, broadening its efforts to address an issue that, if not addressed effectively, would have a very negative impact on its sustainability as a business in Hong Kong. While CLP pursued a conventional approach to engaging lawmakers, regulators, NGOs, and the media around its strategy to reduce Hong Kong's air pollution, it also decided to have a relationship with customers beyond one that had been traditionally transactional.

CLP's decision to contribute actively to address all elements responsible for Hong Kong's air pollution certainly means it has "dealt itself in" on issues over which it has limited influence only, especially the polluted air emanating from the Mainland that presses against the Hong Kong skyline. But in terms of its stakeholders, it is able to position itself as a corporation that is seriously committed not only to the improvement of Hong Kong's air quality, but also to making a difference to all the factors that contribute to it—even though it is not solely responsible for Hong Kong's poor air quality.

On the supply side, it has made commitments to lower its own emissions, invest internationally in renewable energy sources, and offer a commercial service in Mainland China to assist companies there to reduce their demand for electricity. On the demand side, it has identified its customers as important stakeholders who can also act to mitigate Hong Kong's air pollution and, in doing so, may contribute also to altering CLP's business model in the city.

Contributor to air pollution	Stakeholder	Action
CLP and Hong Kong Electric Company	Hong Kong Electric Company, government and regulators, employees, customers, NGOs, media	• Commitment to reduce markedly its own carbon emissions in Hong Kong and its other markets, outlined in its 2009 Energy Vision emissions reduction plan, establishing emission reduction targets out to 2025 • Engagement around its targets with customers, NGOs, government, employees, regulators, and customers • Regular reporting on progress toward reducing emissions
Emissions from Pearl River Delta in China	Mainland Chinese energy generators and users, Chinese governments and regulators, Hong Kong–owned factories operating in Pearl River Delta	Established an energy–efficiency service company in Pearl River Delta that provides services to factories in Shenzhen (over the border) to reduce their energy consumption—aimed primarily at Hong Kong companies operating there
Emissions from motor vehicles in Hong Kong (there are an estimated 600,000 motor vehicles, though many thousands more enter and leave daily from Mainland China)	Motor vehicle drivers, CLP customers, government and regulators, employees, NGOs, and the media	CLP is a public advocate of, and is commercially committed to, widespread use of electric motor vehicles in Hong Kong. It is working closely with local authorities, NGOs, public institutions, and customers to champion and provide infrastructure for electric motor vehicles.
Air pollution from economic activity in Hong Kong	Customers (including small and medium enterprises), government and its agencies, regulators' employees, NGOs, the media	• Concerted energy efficiency education and demonstration program aimed at residential and small and medium enterprise customers • Concerted energy efficiency program for schools, contributing to embedding energy–efficiency behavior among young people, which can also be an element in how a family or smaller enterprise approaches energy use

EXECUTION: ENGAGING CUSTOMERS TO ADDRESS HONG KONG'S AIR POLLUTION

CLP's Group Public Affairs management team believed strongly that having a relationship with customers that was more than just transactional in nature—by enjoining them to be part of efforts to improve air quality—was not only important to addressing the issue, but would also send a strong message to other stakeholders (including government and NGOs) that the company was broadening its efforts beyond what it could do at its power plants.

The message the company sent to all stakeholders by engaging customers as stakeholders was, to paraphrase: "We are a business that is part of the community. We want to continue to be part of the community where we are based and where our people live and work. So, we feel we have a responsibility to look beyond our impact alone, and look at how we assist others to do their bit as well."

As the management function with the most contact with, and knowledge of, CLP's Hong Kong customers, the Marketing and Customer Services division was the vehicle through which direct engagement with customers occurred. The company's efforts are ongoing. But initially, it focused on engaging existing and potential customers with three specific initiatives that it believed would contribute most to reducing Hong Kong's air pollution, and at the same time contribute to securing CLP's long-term sustainability as a profitable and viable electricity generator. Three of these initiatives involved engaging customers as stakeholders to reduce their demand for electricity:

1. A concerted energy efficiency education program in schools aimed at embedding energy efficiency behavior in young people, which could influence the behavior of their families at home.
2. Using CLP's nine retail outlets in Hong Kong and its marketing expertise to encourage customers to purchase energy-efficient appliances. Since 2009, CLP's marketing

approach in its retail outlets has focused on selling the concept of energy efficiency, rather than simply seeking profit from selling appliances.

3. Targeting its commercial customers and the estimated 200,000 small and medium enterprises in Hong Kong—including restaurants, small manufacturers, retailers, and service providers—on how they can save money by using electricity more efficiently and effectively. A by-product of better energy efficiency is less demand for electricity.

The fourth area in which CLP decided to engage customers as stakeholders was more surprising, but highly strategic—its advocacy and demonstration programs to encourage widespread use of electric motor vehicles in Hong Kong.

CLP'S ELECTRIC MOTOR VEHICLE BUZZ

CLP has been quietly promoting electric motor vehicles since the 1990s. However, the evolution of technology since 2008 (better and longer electric battery life) means electric motor vehicles are a far more viable option than in the past. Almost one third of Hong Kong's air pollution is generated by fossil fuel-powered motor vehicles.

The Hong Kong government is the city's primary proponent of electric vehicles. However, CLP is also a major advocate and has been supportive of the government's aspirations for mass electric vehicle use. CLP has determined that it is well placed to encourage its customers and all residents of Hong Kong to consider electric vehicles as a viable alternative, by encouraging its customers and the wider community to consider purchasing electric vehicles, demonstrating vehicle performance, and providing charging station infrastructure.

The company's Group Public Affairs division is engaging NGOs, government agencies, and other stakeholders on the role electric vehicles can play in reducing air pollution, while its Marketing and Customer Services division is leading the engagement directly with customers. The company sees its customers—with whom it has existing relationships—as key stakeholders in shifting community attitudes about electric motor vehicles.

CLP has begun to transition its own fleet of 200 gasoline-powered vehicles to electric vehicles. However, while this transition is important in and of itself to the company, CLP believes it has the marketing and promotional expertise to make a much greater impact. In late 2010, it organized, funded, and managed a five-day electric vehicle demonstration show at Hong Kong's Science Park, where participants could see electric vehicles in action—including a double-decker bus, a motorcycle, a racing car, and electric trucks. The demonstration event included about 50 electric vehicles and an electric vehicle "parade." About 60,000 people attended the demonstration, and 6,000 people drove or rode in electric vehicles as part of the company's efforts to introduce its customers, potential customers, and the wider community to the viability of electric vehicles.

CLP's Group Public Affairs used its media relations expertise and engagement with other stakeholders, including NGOs and government, to generate media and stakeholder interest in and reporting of the show. Part of CLP's engagement with its customers regarding electric vehicles includes communicating that the company has already installed 26 electric vehicle charging stations in the city that can charge vehicles within two hours. The company has also constructed two "quick charge" stations that can power up vehicles in under 20 minutes. As of mid-2011, four additional CLP quick-charge stations were in the planning stage.

CLP believes that Hong Kong's relatively small geographic area makes it ideal for electric vehicles. The company estimates that most road trips are under 50 kilometers. The current generation of electric vehicle batteries last for about 100 kilometers. The company estimates that its customers and other Hong Kong residents could be enticed to purchase electric vehicles if they were affordable, and if customers were confident there was a charging station within ten kilometers of wherever they were in the city.

CLP's approach to collaborating with customers, government, and NGOs also led the company to manage a half-day electric vehicle demonstration program (through one of the Hong Kong Chamber's peak business associations) for senior business people, so that business and community leaders had firsthand experience of driving and traveling in electric vehicles. It has also leased five electric vehicles for use by the city's housing authority, its Science Park, and car rental companies. CLP has communicated with its customers about electric vehicles by using its billing channel—by including promotional materials and information in its electricity bills.

CHILDREN, CHICKENS, AND AIR QUALITY

As noted earlier, another focus of CLP's engagement with its customers as stakeholders in addressing Hong Kong's air pollution is seeking to harness the enthusiasm and influence of children to better understand how energy efficiency can be good for their families and the environment.

The company interacts with primary and secondary school students via a fitted-out "echo bus," which is effectively a mobile classroom designed to educate young people about what they and their families can do to reduce their carbon footprint. As part of CLP's school education program, senior CLP executives have been drafted as "ambassadors" and participate in school visits. The company has also sought to engage its future customers by managing a school-based energy efficiency competition involving secondary schools across Hong Kong. (One of the more quirky elements of the school energy efficiency program includes a message to children to encourage their parents and grandparents not to play mahjong at night, but to conserve energy and lower electricity costs by playing during the day.)

To reach as many young people as possible with its energy efficiency and environmental sustainability message and resources,

CLP developed specific social media channels and platforms, including competitions to encourage ideas for energy conservation (one CLP user-generated energy efficiency video competition targeted at young people reached 40,000 online users as the homemade videos went viral).

As well as engaging customers with electric vehicle advocacy, and indirectly via schools and education programs, CLP sees its commercial customers (especially smaller enterprises) as stakeholders in mitigating air pollution through their use of electricity. Hong Kong is a significant regional headquarters to many large multinational and local corporations that have the capital capacity to meet the costs of installing energy-efficient systems and equipment. When considering the causes of air pollution in the city, CLP identified small and medium enterprise customers as stakeholders who could potentially contribute to lowering Hong Kong's energy emissions—if they had a price motivation and ready advice to do so.

In late 2010, CLP partnered with government agencies, professional associations, contractors, academia, and trade union and environmental groups to establish a "green club" (Green Plus) to work with smaller enterprises to reduce their energy consumption and costs without negatively affecting production. CLP's rationale for engaging its business customers as air pollution stakeholders (shared by environmental public policy advocates and small business groups) was that many smaller enterprises were not engaged with the concept of energy efficiency and frequently lacked capital capacity to meet the upfront costs that could be involved in achieving longer-term reductions in electricity costs. Green Plus offers smaller enterprises and non-profit organizations energy audits, efficiency and consumption analysis and consulting, and energy efficiency training for electrical contractors who work with smaller enterprises and not-for-profits.

CLP estimates the average small enterprise could make energy efficiency cost savings of between five per cent and 20 per cent each year and reduce annual greenhouse gas emissions per small business customer by about 20 tons. A good example of this approach in action is CLP using Green Plus—using seminars and its own marketing channels and direct customer service contact—to encourage thousands of customers in the restaurant business to use LED lighting and capture the steam they use in cooking to heat water. CLP has framed this engagement with restaurants in terms of reducing costs and saving money, advising them that a typical investment in new equipment that is more energy efficient has a payback period of about 18 months. After that, electricity cost savings go directly to the financial bottom line.

CLP cites also how its engagement with customers to cut pollution saved a Hong Kong chicken farm half of its annual electricity bill. Through the Green Plus program, the chicken farmer was advised that his farm's separate cooling and heating systems could be modified to cut his electricity bill and thus reduce energy consumption. Green Plus told him how heat pump technology could extract air from the cooling process (needed as part of egg incubation) and convert it to heat that is needed to warm young chicks.

Through engaging small business customers as stakeholders in a bigger issue (reducing air pollution), CLP is using economic efficiency and cost arguments as well as advocacy as a platform to achieve its purposes. CLP would not put it in these terms, but targeting enlightened self-interest can be a very powerful driver of behavior—especially in small business.

KEY LESSONS: A WORK IN PROGRESS, BUT MUCH HAS BEEN LEARNED

Most CLP senior executives would bristle at any suggestion that the company is making significant progress to reduce Hong Kong's air pollution problems. Instead, they would rightly agree that they have broadened the company's approach to tackling a pressing community issue (that by its very nature is a business issue also) beyond what it can do within its own operations.

From a business viewpoint, CLP is engaging with its customers as stakeholders to address Hong Kong's air pollution woes because it has decided that simply complying with the law, and doing what it has to do legally to reduce its own emissions, is not in the interests of a company that says it wants to be in business for another few centuries. Very few companies have ever "complied" their way to greatness. And in a carbon-constrained world, a big electricity generator and distributor that is doing the bare minimum by simply complying with laws and regulations is not being smart about its future business prospects.

CLP may never win the hearts and minds of every resident in Hong Kong, but that is not what it has set out to do. Of course, CLP—like any responsible company—should be concerned about its reputation: a poor corporate reputation over a sustained period equates to a company placing a giant billboard above its headquarters reading "Come and beat us up. Walk all over us. No one will care."

From an objective management viewpoint, CLP recognizes that the Hong Kong community in which it operates sees it as contributing to a big community problem. It has undertaken to reduce its emissions beyond any legal requirement by changing its operations, and it has committed to reporting publicly on its performance. But from the same viewpoint, CLP has also sought to engage with a spectrum of stakeholders to address the electricity demand side. And it has judged that by engaging its customers as members of the community with a stake in improving air quality, it can potentially empower its customers to take action individually.

CLP's advocacy and support of the government's electric vehicle aspirations are especially interesting. By engaging its customers as it advocates for Hong Kong residents to use electric vehicles *en masse*, CLP has skin in the game in not only reducing its own emissions, but in encouraging one of its most important stakeholder groups to do the same. Its electric vehicle advocacy (including through demonstrations in its electric vehicle show) aligns with its engagement of small business customers to reduce their electricity bills and at the same time reduce carbon emissions; it also aligns with its efforts in schools to embed energy efficiency as second nature in young people.

CLP's challenges as an energy generator are not unique. However, what is not run-of-the-mill is the company's strategy to extend its relationship with customers beyond the transactional, and to engage them to act in their own interests—in a manner that is also likely to make sure more people can see, and be healthy in, their fragrant harbor.

◆ KEY TAKEAWAYS ◆

- As an electricity generator and distributor burning fossil fuels, China Light & Power (CLP) in Hong Kong is blamed by many individuals and groups in the community for the city's serious air pollution problems.
- CLP has acknowledged it does contribute to air pollution in Hong Kong. As well as committing to reducing its own emissions through recalibrating its operations (and reporting publicly on progress and performance), the company believes its own sustainability is linked with the sustainability of Hong Kong. It has decided, therefore, to assist the community to address other major sources of air pollution in the city, including air pollution emanating from southern China, motor vehicle emissions, and economic activity in Hong Kong.
- As part of its embedding itself in a "community" response to poor air quality, CLP has engaged its customers as stakeholders in the issue. It is investing in energy efficiency education in schools to engender energy efficiency habits in young people, which they can take home to influence their families, many of whom are CLP customers.

(*Continued*)

- CLP is also advocating publicly, and engaging its customers with, a shift to mass use of electric vehicles in Hong Kong, which could reduce markedly the 30 per cent in emissions that motor vehicles contribute to air pollution in the city.
- The company is also working with other stakeholders to engage its small enterprise customers with energy efficiency advice and services that can save them money, but also reduce electricity demand and thus greenhouse gas emissions.
- CLP has established an energy efficiency advisory company in Mainland China to advise factories in the Pearl River Delta (especially those that are Hong Kong–owned) on how to save money through energy efficiency action. The aim is to have some impact on reducing greenhouse gas emissions from southern China that drift to and envelop Hong Kong.
- CLP has made a judgment that over the longer term, engaging its customers around actions that will reduce greenhouse gas emissions in Hong Kong will contribute to a more sustainable city and bolster CLP's sustainability as a leading company in that city.

3

CHAPTER

Ensuring Corporate Sustainability through Social Responsibility—Diageo and Responsible Drinking

MARK CHONG

Executive Summary

Global and national concerns over the health and social problems associated with alcohol abuse pose a serious challenge to the alcohol industry's license to operate. This chapter shows how Diageo has responded to this challenge in the Asia Pacific region. Recognizing that addressing alcohol's impact on society is critical to its corporate sustainability, Diageo developed an overarching corporate social responsibility program that aimed to raise awareness about responsible drinking. The company's Responsible Drinking activities have shown that corporate social responsibility can enhance corporate reputation and help the company build strategic relationships with stakeholders.

BACKGROUND

A number of socioeconomic factors drive the strong market growth for alcoholic drinks in emerging Asian economies. These include the increased per capita income and urbanization that are creating a large middle class (especially in countries such as China and India) that is channeling disposable income toward aspirational purchases, as well as favorable demographics that make for an increasing legal drinking age population (Lewis and Morales, 2010).

HEALTH AND SOCIAL IMPACTS OF ALCOHOL IN ASIA

For centuries, and in many societies, alcohol has provided pleasure and played a traditional role in ceremonies and family celebrations. However, the misuse of alcohol—which can result in intoxication, dependence (habitual, compulsive, long-term drinking), and even death—can cause harm to individuals and the society in which they live.

According to the World Health Organization (WHO), the harmful use of alcohol can seriously affect public health—it can compromise individual and social development as well as ruin the lives of individuals and families and damage the fabric of communities. Therefore, it is considered to be one of the main risk factors of poor health globally (WHO, 2010).

Economic wealth and alcohol consumption are correlated: as incomes and GDPs rise, the overall volume of alcohol consumption increases. Hence, as Asia becomes more prosperous, more alcohol will be consumed in the region. This rising tide creates market opportunities for alcohol companies in Asia. But given the negative health and social consequences of alcohol abuse, alcohol companies have also had to become increasingly proactive in promoting responsible consumption to preempt policy and taxation changes that could constrain the sale and use of their products (Lewis and Morales, 2010).

REPUTATION OF THE ALCOHOL INDUSTRY

The alcohol industry as a whole is not accorded the same respect as many other industries, as it is perceived to be a "sin" industry that targets underage drinkers and encourages binge drinking (Ainsbury and Grayson, 2011). Even as some companies try to be "responsible" (e.g., by self-regulating their marketing), there are still many "rogue traders" and "freeloaders" (Ainsbury and Grayson, 2011; Dunphy *et al.*, 2007).[1] To complicate matters, there are few credible and "balanced" public policy advocates the alcohol industry can call on to counter the critics (Ainsbury and Grayson, 2011).

Public scrutiny of the alcohol industry is not new. However, this scrutiny intensified worldwide after 2001—this was signaled in a speech given by Dr. Gro Harlem Brundtland (who was then WHO director) that year: "... the large alcohol manufacturers are trying to establish a habit of drinking alcohol at a very young age ... we need to strengthen our work to counter these influences" (Ainsbury and Grayson, 2011).

In Asia, irresponsible alcohol marketing has emerged as a reputational risk issue for alcohol companies. For example, it is common for coffee shops in the region to sell beer without a license, while many supermarkets display beer and stout alongside soft drinks (Lewis and Morales, 2010).

CHALLENGE FROM WORLD HEALTH ORGANIZATION'S GLOBAL STRATEGY TO REDUCE ALCOHOL-RELATED HARM

The marketing of alcohol is subject to varying degrees of government oversight and regulation under consumer protection laws in most countries around the world. However, government regulation in itself is not enough—even the WHO has acknowledged the important self-regulatory role alcohol companies can play in their capacity as developers, producers, distributors, marketers, and sellers of alcoholic beverages (WHO, 2010).

At the 2010 World Health Assembly, the WHO formally adopted a watershed global strategy to tackle alcohol-related harm. It was the first time the 193 nations of the WHO had reached a consensus on a resolution to confront the harmful use of alcohol. The global strategy covers ten policy areas:

1. Leadership, awareness, and commitment;
2. Health services' responses;
3. Community action;
4. Drink-driving policies;
5. Availability of alcohol;
6. Marketing of alcoholic beverages;
7. Pricing policies;
8. Reducing the negative consequences of drinking and alcohol intoxication;
9. Reducing the public health impact of illicit alcohol and informally produced alcohol; and
10. Monitoring and surveillance.

It presents a range of evidence-based policy options and interventions to WHO member states for each of the target areas (WHO, 2010).

The launch of the WHO's global alcohol strategy is a watershed in collective action to address alcohol issues around the world. Together with other major international alcohol companies, Diageo has been proactive in working with WHO member states to help implement the strategy by supporting and contributing to effective policies that reduce harmful drinking (Lewis and Morales, 2010).

CORPORATE SOCIAL RESPONSIBILITY

Businesses are an integral part of society and hence have obligations not just to shareholders but also to a broader group of stakeholders (Freeman, 1984). A company's social responsiveness may signal that it has achieved a "mutualistic" relationship with potentially powerful groups in its environment. In turn, the existence of this "mutualistic" relationship may influence a company's continued ability to operate as well as thwart challenges from its stakeholders (Fombrun and Shanley, 1990; Pfeffer and Salancik, 1978).

When there is a discrepancy between what a company is doing and how the public expects or prefers it to operate, there will be a legitimacy gap (Sethi, 1977). The gap can result from differences of fact, policy, and values (Heath and Palenchar, 2009). And the wider the legitimacy gap, the more strongly stakeholders will disapprove of the company (Kruckeberg and Starck, 1988) and thus jeopardize its license to operate.

Companies can sustain their long-term ability to create shareholder value only if they obtain broad legitimacy in the societies where they operate (Bonini *et al.*, 2009). Hence, companies constantly need to ensure that their activities—including the nature of their input and output and the manner in which the output is distributed—are congruent with the goals of the society in which they operate. By adapting proactively to these norms and values, a company can preempt legal and regulatory action and thus enjoy greater flexibility in its operations at a lower institutional cost (Sethi, 1975). Companies must also align themselves with stakeholder expectations in order to prevent damage to their reputation (Bertels and Peloza, 2008).

Corporate social responsibility (CSR) has increasingly become the means by which companies align themselves with stakeholder expectations and bolster corporate reputation (Fombrun *et al.*, 2000). Indeed, CSR has become so central to a firm's reputation that the question now is *how* best to do CSR, instead of *whether* or not to do it at all (Smith, 2003). According to Epstein (2008), four main factors are driving companies globally to recognize the critical importance of managing and controlling their corporate social and environmental performance:

1. **Regulations**: Companies increasingly find that they need to address sustainability to satisfy government regulations and industry codes of conduct.

2. **Community relations**: Good performance on sustainability can garner a positive corporate reputation that in turn helps companies to gain the license to operate from governments, communities, and other stakeholders.
3. **Cost and revenue imperatives**: Sustainability can create corporate value by enhancing revenues and lowering costs. In short, sustainability just makes good business sense.
4. **Societal and moral obligations**: Leading organizations recognize the close relationship between business success and a society's well-being.

CSR and sustainability programs can create value for companies by enhancing corporate reputation. More specifically, a company's reputation for environmental, social, and governance programs that go beyond regulatory requirements or industry norms and that meet community needs can—at least partly—help companies achieve financially valuable objectives such as regulatory settlements, a reduced risk of boycotts, and higher retention of talent (Bonini *et al.*, 2009).

According to a 2009 study, 99 sustainability companies that excelled in promoting social well-being and protecting the environment while preserving shareholder value outperformed the broader market by an average of ten per cent over a three-month period during the 2008 financial crisis, and by 15 per cent over a six-month period in the same year (A.T. Kearney, 2009).

DIAGEO

Diageo is the world's leading premium drinks business, and it creates value for its shareholders by manufacturing, packaging, and responsibly marketing branded alcohol—spirits, wine, and beer—on an international scale. Diageo is headquartered in London, and its products are sold in approximately 180 countries worldwide. The company is ranked by the *Financial Times* among the 160 largest companies in the world.

Diageo's business is divided into four key regions: North America, Europe, International, and Asia Pacific. Its global priority brands are its primary growth drivers across its markets and, as such, are the main focus of its business—they include Johnnie Walker, Smirnoff, Baileys, Captain Morgan, Jose Cuervo, J&B, Tanqueray, and Guinness. Together, these brands have the greatest current and future earnings potential and account for approximately 57 per cent of Diageo's global volumes.

THE STAKEHOLDER LANDSCAPE

Customers

Diageo's customers comprise the companies that distribute and sell its products. Diageo shares its sustainability ambitions with many of its customers in various regions. To date, it has worked with its customers to promote responsible drinking and reduce its environmental impact through the development of sustainable packaging and encouragement of recycling. Such programs have in turn helped many Diageo customers reach their own supply chain targets with a social and environmental agenda.

Governments

Alcohol is one of the most regulated industries in the world, with all aspects of the value chain—from production (and product definitions) to sales and marketing, retail, and consumption—subject to varying degrees of legislation or oversight by government authorities. Accordingly, Diageo engages either directly or indirectly through industry trade associations and with governments around the world on aspects of regulation.

Diageo's ability to create a more valuable role for alcohol in society depends to a great extent on a balanced regulatory framework that provides a strong foundation for its programs—especially one that is based on the best evidence, targets specific at-risk populations, treats all forms of alcohol equitably, and involves all stakeholders.

In developed countries that have strong government oversight of markets, regulation and laws relating to the sale of alcoholic beverages are relatively more established. However, in Asia, regulations surrounding alcohol sale continue to develop as some emerging economies experiment with alcohol-related legislation. Many in these countries also face the additional challenge of monitoring and controlling the production, import, and sale of alcoholic beverages, making enforcement of regulations more difficult.

In countries where an appropriate legislative framework is in place, efforts by alcohol companies to change attitudes and reduce alcohol misuse are more effective. A clear national policy on alcohol can improve the effectiveness of initiatives by addressing systemic problems and clarifying issues. Diageo has addressed this issue by establishing consensus on alcohol policy issues, such as responsible marketing, drink-drive blood alcohol content levels, legal purchase age, tax policy, and other regulatory measures (e.g., how to deal with illicit alcohol).

STRATEGIES AND EXECUTION

To effectively address a social issue such as irresponsible drinking, organizations need to engage various stakeholders. Diageo recognized early that if alcoholic beverages were consumed irresponsibly, stakeholders could see its business as part of the problem and thus threaten its license to operate. Moreover, if health risks go unchecked, the families of the company's employees, suppliers, and consumers could be endangered, thus threatening Diageo's long-term viability. Hence, Diageo identified alcohol in society—that is, raising awareness about responsible drinking and aspiring to change consumer attitudes and behavior—as one of its key priorities.

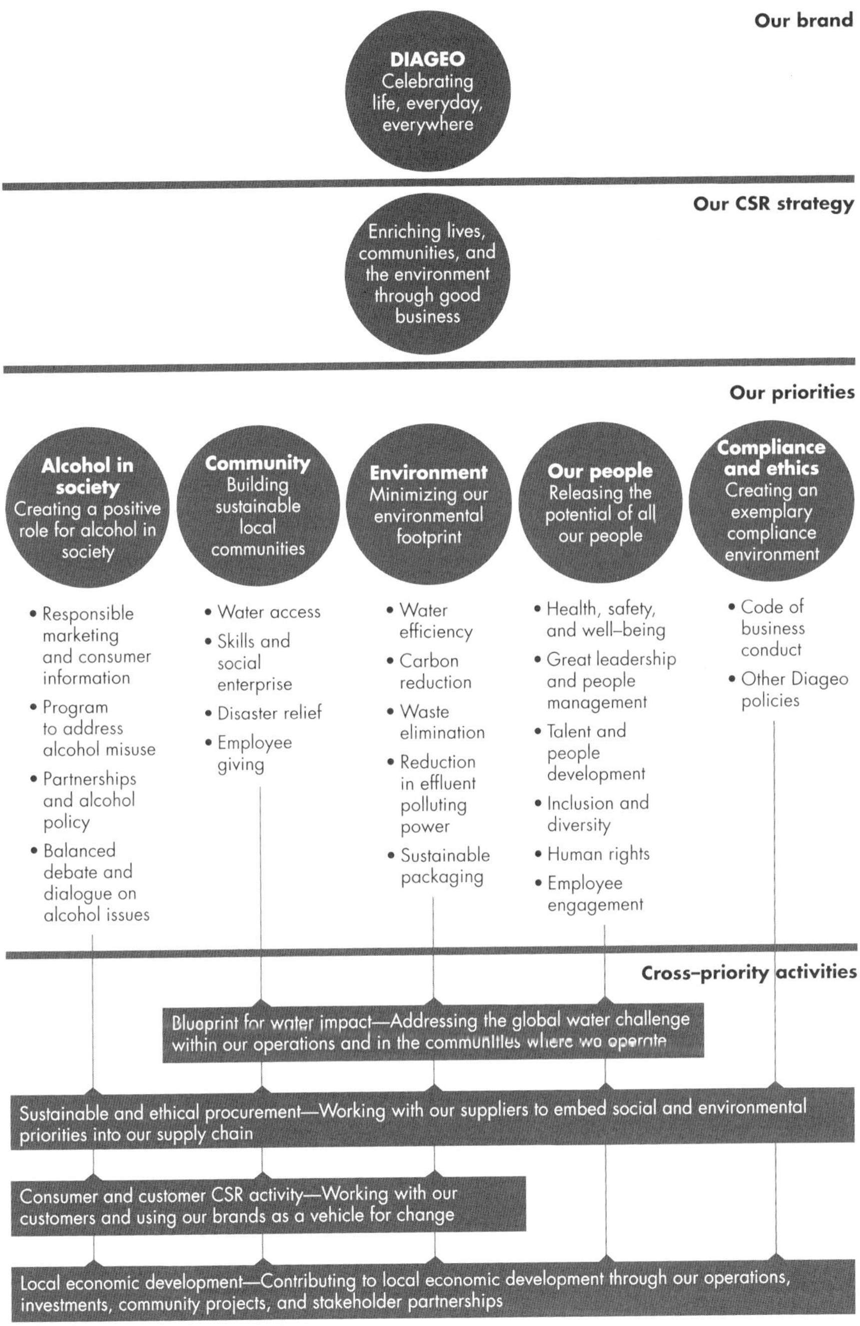

Source: Courtesy of Diageo

THE RESPONSIBLE DRINKING PROGRAM

Alcohol's role in and impact on society is critical to the sustainability of Diageo's business. To address the problem of alcohol misuse, Diageo has identified three areas where it believes it can create the most impact:

1. Set high company and industry standards in responsible marketing and provide consumer information about its brands;
2. Implement initiatives designed to raise awareness and work with others to change attitudes and behavior to minimize alcohol misuse; and
3. Promote effective and targeted alcohol policies and foster balanced debate and stakeholder dialogue at the global, regional, and country levels.

One: Responsible Marketing and Consumer Information

Diageo has instituted a self-regulated marketing code that governs every element of the research, development, and marketing of its brands in all markets where it operates. In addition to the marketing code, Diageo maintains a Digital Code of Practice, which provides detailed guidance on responsible marketing in the digital space. One of the codes, for example, stipulates that Diageo marketing content can appear only where at least 70 per cent of users can reasonably be expected to be above the legal purchase age.

The company also works with bodies that oversee industry and co-regulation codes to encourage public complaints about inappropriate alcohol marketing, and to foster public communication about the resolution of these complaints.

Diageo's success in responsible marketing can be seen in the number of complaints regarding alcohol companies' marketing upheld from 1 July 2009 to 3 June 2010 by the Alcohol Beverages Advertising Code (ABAC), the Advertising Standards Authority for Ireland (ASAI), the Advertising Standards Authority (ASA), the Portman Group, and the Distilled Spirits Council of the United States (DISCUS):

Agency	Brand of alcohol	Complaints
ABAC (Australia)	Diageo brands	1
	All alcoholic beverages	10
ASAI (Ireland)	Diageo brands	0
	All alcoholic beverages	0
ASA (United Kingdom)	Diageo brands	0
	All alcoholic beverages	5
Portman Group (United Kingdom)	Diageo brands	0
	All alcoholic beverages	5
DISCUS (United States)	Diageo brands	0
	All alcoholic beverages	1

Source: Diageo Corporate Citizenship Report 2009

Two: Changing Attitudes and Behavior to Address Alcohol Misuse

In 2010, Diageo supported more than 200 programs in more than 40 countries to address alcohol misuse, either directly or with the support of other organizations. Diageo's local business units have the autonomy to determine their major alcohol-related issues and select a program that suits local circumstances. These programs include Diageo's own DRINKiQ, Johnnie Walker "Join the Pact," Guardian Angels, Cool Drinker, and Better Nights, as well as those developed by DrinkWise and supported by Diageo and other companies.

DRINKWISE

In 2003, intense lobbying by critics of the alcohol industry in Australia resulted in a landmark New South Wales Alcohol Summit that was held in the State Parliament in Sydney. This summit received a surge of media attention that intensified public and political concerns about alcohol abuse (in particular underage drinking) and law and order issues. These concerns escalated into a call for action by state and federal health bureaucrats.

Given this climate, the threat of government intervention "in the public interest"—in the form of new regulations and taxes—appeared imminent. Recognizing that one company acting or lobbying alone would be insufficient to prevent increasing scrutiny and forestall government legislation, Diageo Australia's Managing Director at that time galvanized the industry to develop a concerted responsible drinking campaign (Ainsbury and Grayson, 2011).

Thanks to these efforts, beer, wine, and spirit companies, hoteliers, and liquor retailers, as well as respected members of the community and government came together to form DrinkWise Australia—a not-for-profit organization focused on promoting a safer and healthier drinking culture in the country. The Australian government funded the program to the tune of AU$5 million from 2005 to 2009. Since late 2009, DrinkWise has been entirely supported by voluntary contributions.

An independent benchmark study conducted in 2009 for the first DrinkWise campaign—"Kids Absorb Your Drinking"—revealed the following:

1. A third of all parents (who consumed alcohol) reported that during the last 12 months they had either reduced the amount of alcohol consumed in front of their children (27 per cent) or stopped drinking in front of their children (six per cent);

2. Over four in ten of these parents (41 per cent) indicated that they had reduced their drinking as they wanted to be a good role model and/or set a good example; and
3. Fourteen per cent indicated that TV advertising had been a factor in their decision to cut down or stop drinking in front of their children (http://www.drinkwise.com.au).

In a government marketing study undertaken by Colmar Brunton Social Research in 2009, "Kids Absorb Your Drinking" was the most recalled advertisement of the 30 advertisements studied (http://www.drinkwise.com.au).

The second DrinkWise campaign—"Kids and Alcohol Don't Mix"—enjoyed widespread national newspaper, television, and radio coverage. At the campaign launch at Parliament House in November 2009, the Australian government publicly commended DrinkWise for being a positive move by the alcohol industry to combat binge drinking and a good example of how the community could work together to change the risky drinking culture (http://www.drinkwise.com.au).

DRINKiQ

DRINKiQ was originally developed to raise Diageo employees' "collective drink IQ"—that is, to enhance their understanding of the choices they make as consumers of alcohol. The program brings together tools and information from the best programs—not just Diageo's—for stakeholders who are interested in promoting responsible drinking.

To date, DRINKiQ has been presented to over 1,000 employees across Asia Pacific and to over 18,000 employees around the world (Diageo Corporate Citizenship Report 2010). These employees have, in turn, become ambassadors for responsible drinking to the outside community. In fact, Diageo has extended the DRINKiQ workshop to a range of external stakeholders such as

Source: Courtesy of Diageo

government officials, sports teams, business partners, parents, educators, law enforcers, and retailers. In Asia last year, the program was delivered to external stakeholders in China, India, Korea, and Thailand.

In 2008, Diageo launched the global DRINKiQ website (www.drinkiq.com) to complement the workshops. On the website are experts' views, facts about alcohol, responsible drinking tips, nutrition information about Diageo brands, and an outline of Diageo's approach to responsible drinking. In addition to the global site, there are also a total of 18 country sites, including China, India, Taiwan, and Singapore.

Two key factors set DRINKiQ apart from other responsible drinking programs, said Ron Ainsbury, founder of consulting company Jacaranda and Visiting Fellow at the Cranfield School of Management:

1. A lot of programs start with the premise of: "I think you have a drinking problem and we need to solve your

problem for you." DRINKiQ starts with: "Most of us enjoy having a drink. And those of us who enjoy having a drink would just like to know how we could continue to enjoy it as opposed to having a night we would regret."

2. DRINKiQ is a conversation: "The whole thrust of the session is interaction. The people who run the sessions are called facilitators, not teachers or instructors. They are there to help the conversation. The people attending DRINKiQ have not been preached to. They have not been judged. They are treated like adults. And they feel much more empowered to make a decision" (personal interview).

JOIN THE PACT

Involving the Johnnie Walker sponsorship of the Vodafone McLaren Mercedes Formula One racing team, "Join the Pact" is the latest Johnnie Walker Responsible Drinking campaign. Launched during the 2008 Formula One Grand Prix in Singapore and supported by the Singapore Traffic Police, "Join the Pact" focused on encouraging consumers to sign a pact not to drink and drive and to designate a driver.

In March 2008, a crowd of over 10,000 watched as former F1 world champion and Johnnie Walker Global Responsible Drinking Ambassador Mika Häkkinen demonstrated the importance of staying in control behind the wheel by taking both the Vodafone McLaren Mercedes F1 car and the Mercedes AMG car through expert maneuvers, burnouts, and spins during a two-hour event.

Diageo also installed Johnnie Walker display stands equipped with computer terminals that played a clip of world champion Lewis Hamilton encouraging customers to sign the screen with a stylus, thus committing them to the pact.

Source: Courtesy of Diageo

Since its introduction in Singapore, Diageo has launched "Join the Pact" in China, Malaysia, and Thailand. To date, millions of people around the world have signed up for this pact.

COOL DRIVER

Koreans are known to be generous in their alcohol consumption. While the incidence of drink driving has decreased over the years—the number of drink and drive violations decreased by about 30 per cent from 2008 to 2010, according to the statistics of the National Police Agency—the number of violations remains an issue (e-mail correspondence with Kwon Soo Jin, Diageo Korea).

In 2005, Diageo introduced a responsible drinking campaign called "Cool Drinker" in Korea—the first by any alcohol company in the country—together with the Citizens' Coalition for Safety.

Source: Courtesy of Diageo

The campaign later developed into "Cool Driver," a nationwide program for driving centers, universities, companies, and holiday resorts that has resulted in more than 40,000 consumers pledging not to drink and drive—that is, to be a "Cool Driver" (Diageo Asia Pacific Corporate Citizenship Review 2009).

In 2008, Diageo Korea launched the "Slow Slow Quick Quick" Cool Driver campaign, which encouraged consumers to "drink slowly or less, and head home earlier." The campaign won the 2008 Korean Traffic Safety Award. From November 2010 through February 2011, Diageo's Cool Driver campaign advertisement was exposed to 1.8 million moviegoers in Lotte Cinemas in Seoul (e-mail correspondence with Kwon Soo Jin, Diageo Korea).

GUARDIAN ANGEL

Tackling drink driving is the goal of Diageo's Guardian Angel campaign, which uses a non-preachy, direct communication approach and local celebrities to spread the responsible drinking message. It is designed to remind consumers that drinking sensibly—and, in particular, nominating a driver when they go out—is a matter of personal responsibility and not one that should be left to their "guardian angel."

Launched in Venezuela in 2006, the campaign has run in 14 more countries in Latin America and Asia. Following the activation of the campaign in China, 77 per cent of consumers surveyed said

Source: Courtesy of Diageo

they would be more likely to consider their drinking behavior (Diageo Corporate Citizenship Report 2009).

BETTER NIGHTS

Diageo Australia launched "Better Nights"—a staff training program—in conjunction with the Australian Hostels Association (New South Wales) and ClubsNSW in 2010. The program is based on a DVD that provides practical advice and tips to bar staff on how to deal effectively with alcohol misuse and customer disturbance. Strong evidence in Australia and overseas has shown the effectiveness of this type of training in helping to reduce alcohol-related customer issues in bars. The Diageo sales force shared the Better Nights program at more than 4,000 venues across New South Wales and nationally.

Three: Alcohol Policy and Stakeholder Dialogue

Diageo's sustainability depends in part on its ability to establish consensus on alcohol policy issues such as responsible marketing, drink drive blood alcohol content levels, legal purchase age, tax policy, and other regulatory measures (e.g., dealing with illicit alcohol).

So, together with nine other international alcohol companies, Diageo funds the International Center for Alcohol Policies (ICAP)—a think tank that aims "to reduce the abuse of alcohol worldwide through dialogue and partnerships involving the alcoholic beverage industry, governments, the public health community, and others with an interest in alcohol policy." Self-regulation, drink driving, and non-commercial alcohol are currently the major areas of focus (http://www.icap.org). Through its 2009 book, *Working Together to Reduce Harmful Drinking*, ICAP provided input into the WHO's global strategy to reduce the harmful effects of alcohol (Lewis and Morales, 2010).

KEY LESSONS

Building Corporate Reputation

When a company develops a reputation for strong performance on social, environmental, and governance issues, it can build the trust that is necessary to secure a voice in discussions with regulators (Bonini *et al.*, 2009). By showing its seriousness in helping to develop a responsible drinking culture in the various markets, Diageo has been able to gain acceptance as a legitimate player in the debate on alcohol in society. This, in turn, has helped the company gain the credibility needed to establish strategic partnerships with strong local partners.

In Vietnam, for example, Diageo's reputation for CSR has helped the company establish a strategic partnership with the Hanoi Liquor Company (HALICO). Said HALICO Director, Ho Van Hai, "CSR has increasingly become a key component of HALICO's business strategy. Diageo's reputation for best practice in CSR has provided us with a strategic partner with whom we can share and mutually develop our sustainability agenda in Vietnam" (personal interview, 2011).

Building Industry Partnerships

To bring about change, it is important to work as an industry with a multipronged approach. After all, a company's reputation is often confounded with that of its industry peers (Bertels and Peloza, 2008). Moreover, the negative actions of a single firm may catalyze negative stakeholder reactions that profoundly destabilize all firms operating in the same industry (Barnett, 2006).

DrinkWise has unified rival alcohol companies across the wine, beer, and spirits categories. This unity has given the industry "one" voice and Diageo greater opportunities to engage with stakeholders (particularly the government). In Korea, Diageo was instrumental in the signing of an industry marketing code by all the international and big domestic alcohol companies. The code signing sends a powerful message to Korean regulators that the alcohol industry is serious about self-regulation, thus providing a viable alternative to overly restrictive regulation.

Nonetheless, it has been a challenge getting local companies in some emerging Asian countries on board. There are several reasons for this:

1. Local companies may shun any association with international alcohol companies, as the latter are the main targets of alcohol industry critics.
2. International alcohol companies such as Diageo make up only a small percentage of the industry in some emerging markets and hence have relatively little influence on the actions of the big domestic players, who may not have the same international perspective.
3. Many local companies view the entry of international alcohol companies into their markets with suspicion and unease.

According to Lin Menuhin, CSR Director for Diageo Asia Pacific, the absence of a unified industry (which includes the local companies) diminishes Diageo's ability to advocate to the government and other stakeholders. Moreover, the highly competitive nature of the market environment undermines the development of institutional frameworks, policies, and initiatives that can benefit the industry as a whole (personal interview, 2011).

Opportunities for CSR to Address Social Problems

There are excellent opportunities for CSR to address social issues and thus grow corporate reputation. In South Korea, for example, alcohol consumption is key to creating group bonding, showing mutual respect, and building trust—this may explain why Korean society is perceived to be tolerant of behaviors associated with excessive alcohol consumption. In order to address this harmful environment, Diageo raised public awareness on the risks associated with irresponsible drinking and became the first company to launch a national responsible drinking program.

CONCLUSION

Alcohol misuse is a social problem that is attracting increasing stakeholder scrutiny in Asia Pacific. While efforts by Diageo and the alcohol industry to encourage responsible drinking continue to be controversial, especially with recent challenges by organizations such as the Australian National Preventative Health Taskforce, they underscore the point that companies must be constant in redoubling their efforts to demonstrate responsibility and genuine societal contribution.

To create a sustainable future for itself and the communities in which it operates, Diageo has taken on a proactive role in addressing alcohol misuse through its Responsible Drinking activities. However, behavioral change takes time—"Rome was not built in a day"—and there is no one-size-fits-all approach in a culturally diverse region such as Asia Pacific. Moreover, alcohol policies in Asia are still in their infancy, a situation that is complicated by limited access to policy makers in some of the Asian markets. Nonetheless, Diageo has shown that through CSR, an organization can engage its key stakeholders, enhance its reputation, and lay the foundations for corporate and societal sustainability.

◆ KEY TAKEAWAYS ◆

- Social issues present companies with excellent opportunities to engage in CSR and thus grow corporate reputation.
- Companies should prioritize social issues that are critical to their own sustainability.
- To effectively address a social issue, companies need to engage various stakeholders.

(*Continued*)

- By developing a reputation for performance on social issues, a company can build the trust that is necessary to secure a voice in discussions with regulators.
- It is important for companies in the same industry to work together—this unity can give the industry "one" voice and thus greater leverage when engaging with stakeholders.

Acknowledgments

The author would like to express his sincere appreciation to Lin Menuhin (Diageo Asia Pacific), Christina Koh (Grayling Asia), Kwon Soo Jin (Diageo Korea), and Ron Ainsbury (Jacaranda) for their kind assistance.

Note

1. A company might go through the following stages or phases on its journey of building sustainable business practices (Dunphy *et al.*, 2007):

   Phase 1: Rejection—the freeloaders and stealthy saboteurs
   Phase 2: Non-responsiveness—the "bunker wombats"
   Phase 3: Compliance—the reactive minimalists
   Phase 4: Efficiency—the industrious stewards
   Phase 5: Strategic proactivity—the proactive strategists
   Phase 6: The sustaining organization—the transformative futurists

References

Ainsbury, R. and Grayson, D. (2011). *DrinkWise: Uniting an Industry*. Cranfield University School of Management case study (Reference no. 711-010-1).

Asia Pacific Corporate Citizenship Review 2009. Retrieved from http://www.diageo.com/Lists/Resources/Attachments/542/APACpercent20CCR09.pdf.

Barnett, M.L. (2006). Finding a working balance between competitive and communal strategies. *Journal of Management Studies*, 43(8), 1753–73.

Bertels, S. and Peloza, J. (2008). Running just to stand still? Managing CSR reputations in an era of ratcheting expectations. *Corporate Reputation Review*, **11**(1), 56–72.

Bonini, S., Koller, T.M. and Mirvis, P.H. (2009). Valuing social responsibility programs. *McKinsey Quarterly*, **4**, 65–73.

Diageo Corporate Citizenship Report 2009. Retrieved from http://www.diageoreports.com/2009/.

Diageo Corporate Citizenship Report 2010. Retrieved from http://ccreport2010.diageoreports.com/.

Dunphy, D., Griffiths, A. and Benn, S. (2007). *Organisational Change for Corporate Sustainability*. London and New York: Routledge.

Epstein, M.J. (2008). *Making Sustainability Work: Best Practices in Managing and Measuring Corporate Social, Environmental, and Economic Impacts*. Sheffield, UK: Greenleaf Publishing.

Fombrun, C.J., Gardberg, N.A. and Barnett, M.L. (2000). Opportunity platforms and safety nets: corporate citizenship and reputational risk. *Business and Society Review*, **105**(1), 85–106.

Fombrun, C. and Shanley, M. (1990). What's in a name? Reputation building and corporate strategy. *Academy of Management Journal*, **33**(2), 233–58.

Freeman, R.E. (1984). *Strategic Management: A Stakeholder Approach*. Boston: Pitman.

Heath, R.L. and Palenchar, M.J. (2009). *Strategic Issues Management: Organizations and Public Policy Challenges*. Thousand Oaks, CA: Sage.

Kearney, A.T. (2009). *"Green Winners." The Performance of Sustainability-focused Companies During the Financial Crisis*. Retrieved from http://www.atkearney.com/index.php/Publications/green-winners.html.

Kruckeberg, D. and Starck, K. (1988). *Public Relations and Community: A Reconstructed Theory*. New York: Praeger.

Lewis, R. and Morales, R.M. (2010). *Beverages in Asia*. Retrieved from www.responsibleresearch.com/Beverages_in_Asia.pdf.

Pfeffer, J. and Salancik, G. (1978). *The External Control of Organizations: A Resource Dependence Perspective*. New York: Harper and Row.

Sethi, S.P. (1975). Dimensions of corporate social performance: an analytical framework. *California Management Review*, **17**(3), 58–64.

Sethi, S.P. (1977). *Advocacy Advertising and Large Corporations: Social Conflict, Big Business Image, the News Media, and Public Policy*. Lexington, MA: D.C. Heath.

Smith, C.N. (2003). Corporate social responsibility: whether or how? *California Management Review*, **45**(4), 52–76.

WHO. (2010). *Strategies to Reduce the Harmful Use of Alcohol: Draft Global Strategy. Sixty-Third World Health Assembly Provisional Agenda Item 11.10*. Retrieved from http://apps.who.int/gb/ebwha/pdf_files/WHA63/A63_13-en.pdf.

CHAPTER 4

Communicating with the Asian Customer—Lessons from the Agrifood Sector

HARVEY GLICK

Executive Summary

The communication landscape has evolved from a one-to-one discussion with customers into a many-to-many conversation. Today, a range of stakeholders have inserted themselves in the communication chain between company and customer, making effective communication with the customer more challenging. As the communication landscape evolves, company communication with customers must also evolve. Communication must not only reflect the needs of the customer, but also address broader societal issues that are important to relevant stakeholders.

In this chapter, I discuss how Monsanto has evolved in its efforts to communicate more effectively with its farmer customers in Asia. I review the range of stakeholders involved in the dialogue—Asian consumers, media, nongovernmental organizations, and civil society—and Monsanto's approach to ensure it maintains a meaningful dialogue with its customers on its company values and products. I also discuss the challenge of measuring the quality of customer communication and metrics for measuring the impact of this process.

BACKGROUND

For a company focused solely on agriculture, the pace at which farming tools and practices are changing sets a communication challenge in itself. But the broader landscape in which we live and do business is changing too—and we need to keep moving with the times.

The name Monsanto has been around since 1901, and throughout its history the company has been involved in products ranging from pharmaceuticals and artificial sweeteners to fibers and protein supplements. The present-day Monsanto Company actually began in 2000, as a spin-off of the original Monsanto Company. A company focused solely on agriculture, it develops and sells seeds and traits developed through plant breeding and biotechnology.

Monsanto was one of the first companies to offer products developed through modern biotechnology to farmers. Since 1996, when the first commercial biotech crops were planted on a large area, farmers' rapid adoption of these crops has made the technology the fastest ever adopted in agriculture. In 2010, the global area planted to crops developed through biotechnology was almost 150 million hectares (James, 2010)—an 87-fold hectare increase since 1996. Today, biotech crops are planted by over 15 million farmers in 29 countries. The majority of these farmers are in Asia, in countries such as China, India, and the Philippines; and the future growth of these technologies is expected to be greatest in the developing nations of Asia.

Monsanto often has direct contact with farmers on their farms as it strives to better understand the latter's problems in growing and marketing their crops for food, feed, and fiber uses. When the first new seed products of modern biotechnology were developed, the company continued to focus on customer communication.

Monsanto knew farmers were benefiting from its new seed products, because the farmers were saying that the technology was adding value to their farming operations in a number of ways. But the company also realized that agriculture as an industry was not well understood by policy makers or the public at large. Many non-farm stakeholders were not seeing the challenges faced by farmers, nor fully appreciating the tremendous achievements farmers were making, in part due to the adoption and use of products developed using modern biotechnology. Increasingly, some consumers began to have their own conversations with the farmer about Monsanto's products. So did many other stakeholders. Activists, civil groups, public sector agencies, faith-based organizations, and others inserted themselves into the communication chain between Monsanto and the farmers. The farmers were getting a lot of information about Monsanto's products from a variety of sources, all filtered through the different-colored lens of each stakeholder.

Thus, the "one-to-one" dialogue Monsanto historically enjoyed with its customers had evolved into a "many-to-many" conversation. Often, the company found that it was not part of these conversations. Its voice was not being heard. It became clear that the corporation needed to engage in a more meaningful dialogue—not only with its customers, but also with this broader group of stakeholders with whom it had not communicated directly in the past. The challenge was to figure out how the company could communicate its vision and values and the benefits of its products.

Billions of people depend on what farmers do. As populations rise, demand for food, feed and fiber will continue to increase. It is estimated that in order to feed an anticipated population of 9.3 billion, farmers will have to grow as much food in the next few decades as they have produced in the past 10,000 years combined. They must accomplish this while overcoming obstacles such as urbanization; scarcity of land; shrinking supplies of water, fuel, and fertilizer; and climate change. The reality is that the world needs more food, and farmers need to produce it more sustainably, on a static land base using fewer resources. Monsanto's stated purpose is to work alongside farmers, to improve their lives by offering them new *choices* of seed as they work to tackle these challenges. The company needed to start proactively explaining that this was what it stood for.

To do this, it had to use modern methods of communication. It was operating in a vastly different landscape than the one faced by a sales representative or communication specialist back in the 1970s. It was now dealing with an increasingly complex environment that was making communication with customers more difficult, but even more critical. In addition, it became imperative for the company to engage in dialogue with the new broader group of stakeholders who had opinions about its products. Monsanto had to embrace the "many-to-many" nature of the conversation and better understand the new communication environment.

THE STAKEHOLDER LANDSCAPE

To do this, the company asked itself: "Who are these stakeholders who have such an influential role in the communication with the farmer customer?" The answer was that the stakeholders included many different groups with whom Monsanto had no active dialogue, who had little or no connection to agriculture, had a minimal understanding of the science of biotechnology, and had few opportunities to interact or engage in dialogue with Monsanto or even its farmer customers.

The Consuming Public

Our global society is becoming increasingly urban, with more people living in cities. This trend is expected to continue, especially in Asia, where the migration from rural village to urban center is a challenge faced by civil planners. One direct result of urbanization is that we now live in a world that is increasingly unaware of sources of food and fiber and is not well-versed in commercial food production practices. A recent survey by the UK organization Linking Environment and Farming found 22 per cent of the 1,000-plus adults questioned did not know bacon and sausages originated from farms.

The survey also found four in ten people did not know yogurt was made using farm produce, nearly half were unaware the raw ingredients for beer started off in farmers' fields, and 23 per cent did not know bread's main ingredients came from the farm. Almost half of the 16- to 24-year-olds questioned had never visited a farm (of which there are 195,000 in England).

A second global trend of importance is the diminishing literacy of science across the general public. Despite the growing dependence on high-tech products such as computers, phones, and other digital technologies, scientific understanding is on the decline. The US National Science Foundation released a report in 2001 showing that while adults claim to be very interested in science, few truly understand what it is all about. In *their* related survey, only about 50 per cent of respondents knew that the earliest humans did not live at the same time as dinosaurs, that it takes Earth one year to orbit the sun, and that electrons are smaller than atoms. Crucially, *from a communications standpoint*, only one-third could adequately explain what it meant to study something scientifically.

This combination of urbanization (which results in a greater separation of people from food production) and decreasing scientific literacy in general creates a challenging environment for communication. Explaining new innovative production technologies such as modern biotechnology is not easy—the science is challenging to understand even for people with a high level of scientific literacy. When you add the emotional and highly personal subject of food, the communication challenge with the public becomes difficult but critical. The combination of all these factors makes this stakeholder vulnerable to non-scientific, misrepresentative information that is communicated with the intent to create concern and fear of the "unknown" about a new food production technology.

Many consumers have strong feelings about how they would like farmers to grow food, although most people are not fully aware of the role farmers play in meeting our food and feed needs. When surveyed, many consumers express a preference for food grown in ways they believe to be more environmentally friendly. But sometimes there is a perception gap between what production methods are the most "sustainable" and what consumers perceive to be the case. The consuming public ultimately makes its demands known at the retail end of the chain by requesting food that is produced more sustainably, and this works its way back up the retail food chain as food manufacturers and food providers must demonstrate they are procuring raw materials such as grains, meat, and vegetables from farms with more "sustainable" production systems. A small portion of customers are even willing to pay a marginal premium for food they perceive to be produced in this way.

Monsanto's Farmer Customers

The Asia Pacific region is heavily dominated by resource-poor farmers, many of whom cultivate areas less than one hectare in size. Across developing Asia, millions of families, particularly those in rural areas, spend more than half of their household income on food. Home to 60 per cent of the world's population and almost 80 per cent of the world's farmers, the region is pressed to raise food productivity and improve agricultural efficiency while conserving environmental resources for future generations.

It is generally accepted that if current climate trends persist, the yields of current irrigated crops in Asia will likely decrease significantly by 2050. The resulting food scarcity will lead to higher prices and reduced caloric intake across the region. The pressures are manifold: a rapidly expanding population, rising demand for food, declining arable land, and a shrinking agricultural labor force.

While farmers vary across Asia, the majority have low incomes and many have little formal education. Farmers in Asia are aging as younger generations follow the trend of urbanization, and fewer young people have aspirations of a career in agricultural food production.

Asian farmers are numerous and have small landholdings, making them a highly fragmented, non-homogeneous group that is difficult to reach. They have numerous languages and dialects that can differ within regions of the same country. Most have limited access to markets, being constrained by local infrastructure such as roads and bridges and the lack of financial infrastructure and affordable credit. Access to the Internet and other online options is also highly variable. While Internet usage is increasing among farmers in Asia, access to these services is limited. Therefore, reaching the farmers and having a meaningful dialogue with them about products and future technological innovations is challenging.

The Media

The role of the media and type of media available varies widely across the region, and the ways to approach the media in each country must be addressed on a case-by-case basis. There is no "one size fits all" model for companies such as Monsanto to reach out to the media to get its message out. Issues of language (and dialect) can be significant in some countries. Many newspapers have a "national" edition that is published in the capital city in the official government language, and this is often targeted at national government officials and opinion leaders. The same newspaper may also have several "regional" publications, written in the local language or dialect. Articles that appear in the national edition may be modified in the local paper or not even appear at all.

There is a constant need to help inform the media, as the global agricultural landscape continues to evolve to meet the challenges and needs of our growing population. As this evolution occurs, it often raises interest, questions, and sometimes concern, especially when it relates to the environment and food. The media are often challenged by trying to learn and report on complex topics such as agriculture, science, and the environment in a limited amount of time to support the 24-hour news cycle. Those opposed philosophically, ethically, or socially to some of the tools farmers are utilizing to produce more food, such as modern biotechnology, have become increasingly adept at using the media to deliver their messages. This is true across many forms of media.

Nongovernmental Organizations and Civil Society

Civil societies are increasingly populated by organizations such as registered charities, development nongovernmental organizations (NGOs), community groups, women's organizations, faith-based organizations, professional associations, trade unions, self-help groups, business associations, coalitions, and advocacy groups. The types of organizations and their roles vary widely across countries based on cultural, legal, and societal norms. In some countries, including the Philippines and Malaysia, faith-based organizations play a very important role in facilitating social discourse on a number of important topics, including food security and food production. NGOs are readily accepted in some countries while merely tolerated in others. In some countries, NGOs, or at least the most activist or protest-oriented ones, are limited in their operation.

NGOs exist for a variety of reasons, usually to further the political or social goals of their members or funders. There are a huge number of such organizations, and their goals cover a broad range of political and philosophical positions, including improving the state of the natural environment, encouraging the observance of human rights, and improving the welfare of the disadvantaged. Some NGOs have other agendas. There are a number of NGOs that share some of Monsanto's visions, including helping farmers produce more and conserve more. But sometimes the company finds itself disagreeing with NGOs about the best ways to accomplish these goals or the safety or benefits of its technologies.

NGOs vary in their methods. Some act primarily as lobbyists, while others conduct programs and activities to help or educate people. But what they all have in common is the need for healthy relationships with the public to meet their goals. Foundations and charities use sophisticated public relations campaigns to raise funds and employ standard lobbying techniques with governments. The more sophisticated ones are truly multinational in scope and content, often operating in more countries and with larger lobbying or advertising budgets than many corporations. They seamlessly transfer information, ideas, programs, and fund-raising techniques across their global organizations. They enjoy access to, and successfully utilize, a wide range of new media—including online social networks—for distributing information that is largely unedited or unfiltered. In doing so, they have obtained remarkable media access and often run sensational, highly charged, emotional campaigns, adding to what is already a challenging communication landscape. Their method often is to define the issue first, co-opt the language and words that are most helpful to their cause, and force all other parties to respond to their framing of the issue. This is a very effective tactic and often means that companies such as Monsanto must first overcome the perception of products that they have created.

Like other stakeholders, different NGOs have different needs, widely varying levels of understanding about science and technology, and varying degrees of access and exposure to the tools needed to communicate effectively. Their operations vary from country to country and even within different regions of the same country.

With these emerging stakeholder groups, the communication landscape had changed significantly and Monsanto's techniques of communicating with customers needed review. The company needed to reevaluate its efforts so that it could better communicate the vision of its company and the value of its products to customers, while also effectively communicating with other stakeholders. Monsanto was not looking for a new communication campaign, but rather an approach that would better fit the new communication landscape it faced.

STRATEGIES: SUSTAINABILITY IN AGRICULTURE—WHAT DOES IT LOOK LIKE?

The common use of the term "sustainability" began with the 1987 report *Our Common Future* published by the World Commission on the Environment and Development. It suggested that sustainable development "meets the needs of the present without compromising the ability of future generations to meet their own needs." Most people would agree that to achieve sustainability, farmers need to get more from every acre of land, every drop of water, and every unit of energy—today and tomorrow.

From 2007 to 2008, Monsanto engaged in two-way dialogue about sustainability with farmers, policy makers, scientists, NGOs, and experts from academia and industry. It received a lot of good feedback, and there was general agreement among all these groups on a number of things, including the idea that in order for agriculture to be sustainable, the environment needed to be protected and even improved so future generations could meet the challenges of their day.

Achieving sustainability is a complex task that involves the entire food production chain. However, it all starts with the farmers, as they are the people who make it happen on their farm. Both large farmers in industrialized countries and small farmers in developing countries must produce sufficiently to keep food and energy affordable while feeding their families. Small farmers, in particular, must create additional income from agriculture to break the cycle of poverty and hunger. Agriculture certainly will not be considered sustainable if the social well-being of nearly one billion farmers is lost in the process.

In 2008, Monsanto sets three fundamental goals to help farmers make agriculture more sustainable. These goals state that by 2030, the company will help farmers to:

1. **Produce more**: Develop improved seeds that help farmers double yields from 2,000 levels for corn, soybeans, cotton, and spring-planted canola.

2. **Conserve more**: Develop seeds that use one-third fewer key resources per unit of output, lessen habitat loss, and improve water quality.
3. **Improve lives**: Help improve the livelihood of farmers and the people who depend on them, including resource-poor farm families in developing Asian countries.

In order to make a difference in many parts of the world, it will take a diverse set of groups working together, including governments, NGOs, and private companies. It will take technology and, most important, it will take cooperation.

EXECUTION: THE ROLL-OUT

The concept of sustainability and sustainable yield evolved slowly and organically within the company. Once the abovementioned three sustainable yield goals were in place, they soon became incorporated internally by Monsanto's employees in thinking about the way to do business. The concept of sustainable agriculture was quickly embraced throughout the organization. These goals guided planning and priorities for Monsanto's research employees as they continued efforts to offer farmers more choice in their efforts to grow more food more efficiently. These sustainability goals also gave employees across the organization—from Legal to Accounting to Human Resources—a better understanding of the company's goals and objectives, its commitment to sustainable agriculture, and how its products would help farmers and global society achieve these important objectives. This is particularly true in the Asia Pacific region.

Each of Monsanto's businesses in the Asia region was encouraged to appoint a sustainability "champion" and to engage a team whose focus was to ensure that all employees understood the following:

1. The extent of the challenges facing Asia Pacific in terms of food production into the future and therefore why the company was shifting its business focus; and

2. What exactly Monsanto was planning to do to help address these challenges.

Field sales representatives in each country began having discussions with farmers about the importance of yield, the impact of climate change, and the urgent need to reduce the amount of water and fertilizer used in the farming operations. They began to explain how Monsanto's products could help farmers begin to achieve these goals.

Monsanto's scientists began conversations with local Asian scientists about the importance of increasing agricultural productivity in the face of climate change, and the need to develop plants better adapted to changing rainfall and temperature patterns. These types of conversations are a critical step in advancing the research and development process where public and private sector collaborations are so important.

Business leaders found that stakeholders across Asia were highly focused on national food security issues and the challenge of maintaining adequate food at affordable prices in the face of looming climate change. Recent public demonstrations in several Asian countries protesting increases in food prices due to production shortfalls had received considerable media attention. It was against this backdrop that stakeholders became more interested and receptive to learn about innovative food production technologies such as modern biotechnology and how these technologies could be part of the solution to achieve long-term food security.

When faced with the goal of attracting, hiring, and retaining new employees, Monsanto's Human Resource team found that the company's commitment to sustainable food production was most helpful in the discussion with prospective new employees. It helped the company articulate its goals and values in a way that was meaningful to a younger, more socially conscious cadre of potential employees and helped provide them with a better understanding of the company and its products.

Employees across the organization have embraced sustainability and organized themselves to ensure that each country developed locally appropriate plans on how to best communicate and achieve these sustainable yield goals through the organizations's business operations. But this was only half the task. Monsanto needed to reach out and engage stakeholders outside the company as well. Many consumers are wary of corporate communication and see it as self-serving and not entirely independent. The company needed to engage credible, independent third parties who could evaluate and validate its strategy and messages on how it could help farmers increase production sustainably. It hoped that the third parties would also be able to increase the amplification and frequency of the message. The first step was to have discussions with a range of scientific experts in many different countries who were all worried about food security, climate change, and the challenge of growing more food with fewer resources, and who were committed to using innovative technological solutions.

Monsanto participated in a broad, multi-sector coalition headed by the Keystone Center in the United States, which conducted an initial study on agricultural sustainability covering four different crops, including corn. This study confirmed that new seed technologies developed through breeding and modern biotechnology were resulting in higher productivity and lower net use of inputs such as water, energy, and pesticides. However, the data was based on farming systems in the United States—which is made up of large, highly technical, well-financed farming operations with a well-developed rural infrastructure. Asian farming systems are quite different, and the question remained whether the same results would be delivered for Asian farmers. Clearly, there was a need to evaluate and substantiate this sustainability message for farmers, consumers, and the media in Asia.

The Philippines has a long history of growing corn incorporating modern biotechnology, and this was one of the countries identified as a useful starting point for evaluating these issues in

Asia. Philippine farmers have been growing genetically modified (GM) corn since 2003. In 2010, more than 270,000 farmers planted more than 500,000 hectares of GM corn. The rapid adoption of GM technology by Philippine farmers was strong empirical evidence that GM corn was providing higher yields with lowered production costs. Nevertheless, opponents of this technology were lobbying and advocating against it.

In 2010, a study published by Dr. Leonardo Gonzales, a leading agricultural economist and president of Skip/Strive Inc.—a not-for-profit foundation in the Philippines—confirmed that the introduction of new technologies developed through breeding and modern biotechnology contributed to higher productivity and better resource use efficiency. According to his study:

1. From 1995 to 2009, aggregate corn production of 4.1 million metric tons increased to seven million metric tons.
2. The use of these products has led to improvements in resource use efficiency in land, human, labor, and fertilizer.
3. From 1975 to 2009, the land required to produce one metric ton of corn grain decreased from 1.163 hectare to 0.382 hectare—a 67.2 per cent land use improvement. In other words, it took 67 per cent less land to grow one metric ton of corn in 2009 compared to 1975.

The results of the Philippine study showed the same results as other studies, but this time the data was more typical of Asian farming systems.

With this additional third-party validation, Monsanto's employees increased the frequency of discussions about sustainable production with all stakeholders. The sustainability messages were included in presentations to farmers, consumers, media, NGOs, and scientists across the region. Equally important, the company's employees gained increased confidence to discuss the values and benefits of their products when speaking with friends and associates in their local communities. Monsanto had created a large and diverse set of employee communicators who were willing and able to amplify a message very effectively with a broad range of stakeholders in an informal—but effective—fashion.

MEASURING SUCCESS

Quantifying the success of any communication initiative is nearly impossible unless one is measuring an indicator such as sales or profit. Even then, it is difficult to determine the exact impact of a specific communication activity. To measure this type of impact, it is important to identify appropriate metrics that can provide an understanding of whether one is increasing the quality of the dialogue and discussion with customers and related stakeholders. These metrics can include—but are not limited to—media interactions (frequency, quality, and accuracy of articles about a company and products); consumer surveys of companies and products; ability to attract and retain top talent; invitations to participate and present at international conferences; and quality of internal employee morale and motivation.

The following examples are given as indicative metrics of the way attitude and understanding have been affected since Monsanto began to talk about sustainable food production in Asia and globally. Based on anecdotal information from a range of stakeholders, it appears that the company's messages about what it is trying to achieve as a business—and how it is communicating its priorities, values, and goals—is starting to resonate with stakeholders.

Consumer Awareness

In 2008, the Asian Food Information Centre (AFIC) conducted a study on the perceptions of consumers in Asia toward food biotechnology. Despite continuing media focus on "food concerns," key findings by AFIC included the following:

1. The common and most important *food safety concerns* are food poisoning, country of origin, and pesticide residues. Food biotechnology is not a top-of-mind concern for consumers and is currently much less of a concern for consumers when compared to other food safety issues. These findings hold true across Asia, with the exception of South Korea.
2. Consumers are very positive toward plant biotechnology when the technology is related to *sustainable food production*. More than 90 per cent of the consumers in China, India, and the Philippines said they supported food production using plant biotechnology to deliver sustainable benefits (growing more food with fewer inputs/resources). In Japan and South Korea—where local agricultural production is less significant—over two-thirds of consumers supported the use of biotechnology to achieve sustainable benefits.

Question: If foods produced through plant biotechnology were able to produce sustainable benefits, would you support the use of biotechnology?

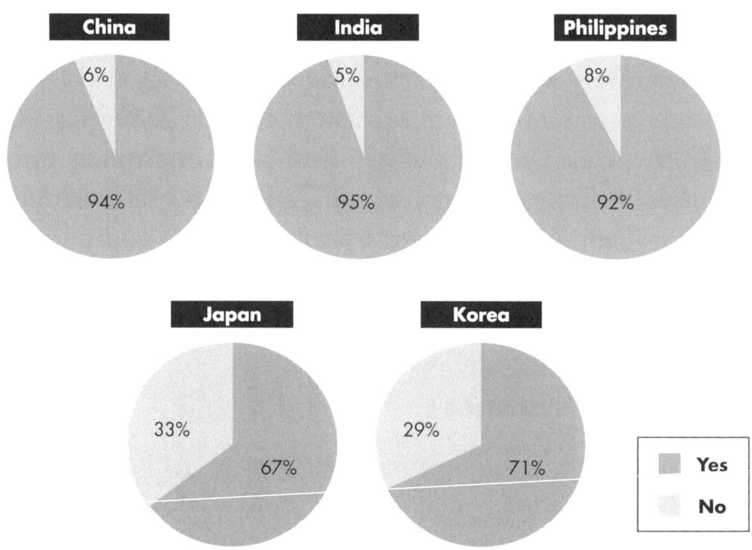

Source: Courtesy of Asian Food Information Centre

Farmer Adoption

Farmers worldwide, both small-scale and large-scale, are rapidly adopting biotech crops due to the benefits of the technology. They understand the challenge of producing food, and the increasing challenge of farming in the face of climate change with reduced availability of inputs such as water and fertilizer. In 2010, 15 million farmers planted 150 million hectares of biotech crops in 25 countries. Notably, in 2010, 14 million of the 15 million farmers (or 90 per cent) were small and resource-poor farmers from developing countries. There has been an 87-fold increase from 1996 to 2010, making modern biotechnology the fastest-adopted crop technology ever.

Farmers have said that by using biotechnology, they believe they are addressing the societal demands of producing food more sustainably, using fewer resources such as water, pesticides, and fertilizer. Many farmers now feel more confident articulating this to the consuming public and other stakeholders.

World Attention to Global Challenges

Over the past three years, several international bodies including the G8, the 2009 FAO Food Summit, the World Economic Forum, and the Royal Society of London have advocated an urgent need for assigning top priority to agriculture, food self-sufficiency and security, and the alleviation of hunger, malnutrition, and poverty. More specifically, given the pivotal role of crops in food, feed, and fiber production, there has been a strong declaration that both conventional and biotech crops should be used to achieve "a substantial and sustainable intensification of crop productivity" on the 1.5 billion hectares of crop land in use today" (James, 2010).

Monsanto's efforts to communicate sustainable food production are still in the early stages. The quality of the dialogue with the company's farm customers has improved, and farmers now feel empowered to articulate how their farming operations are addressing the challenge of sustainable food security. They are more confident in rebutting the attacks of those who disagree with the use of modern biotechnology. Independent and influential international organizations are beginning to engage in the "many-to-many" discussions and are bringing a more balanced and science-based approach to the table when talking about the role of modern breeding and biotechnology. This is providing a counterpoint to the rhetoric that often is put forward by the more extreme stakeholders in this discussion.

Media outlets are beginning to provide more balanced coverage of modern biotechnology and farming in Asia. There is an increased understanding of the impact of climate change on food production and how production shortfalls continue to trigger large price volatility for food products. The need for high-yielding plants from advanced breeding and biotechnology that can adapt to variable rainfall and temperature patterns is increasingly being included in articles.

KEY LESSONS

As a company, Monsanto is constantly evolving. Its customers and stakeholders are also evolving, as are the means available to communicate with them. Delivering timely and accurate information about Monsanto's values and goals as well as its products is difficult in this ever-changing landscape. There is no doubt that with the passing of time, new challenges will arise. The communication landscape will continue to change and evolve. As the challenges facing farmers increase, the general public's understanding of these challenges becomes even more critical.

By clearly articulating the vision of a company, it is possible to have a quality discussion with customers and stakeholders. A sales representative can be given the tools and the confidence to stand in front of a crowd and deliver a message that is pertinent and timely, and one that he is proud to give. It is possible to engage with public-sector scientists in meaningful discussions about research and development priorities and potentially discuss collaborative projects. And it is possible to attract and retain top talents who are committed to sustainable food production and the need to support farmers in meeting the challenges of our growing population.

◆ KEY TAKEAWAYS ◆

- Monitor and assess the quality of the dialogue with your end–customer to see if it is being well received.
- Ensure that employees understand the company mission and core values, and that they are knowledgeable about the company's research and development focus and the value that the company's products provide.
- Identify and understand the impediments that make it difficult to have an honest and open dialogue with customers and other important stakeholders, including the consuming public, nongovernmental organizations, and the media.
- Recognize that today's "many–to–many" communication norms can result in customers receiving a different or distorted view about the company and its products.
- Communicate clearly and accurately the core values of the company and the benefits of its products using a variety of communication channels.

References

Asian Food Information Centre. (2008). *Food Biotechnology—Consumer Perceptions of Food Biotechnology in Asia*. Retrieved from http://www.whybiotech.com/resources/tps/AsiaConsumerPerceptions.pdf.

James, C. (2010). *ISAAA Brief 42: Global Status of Commercialised Biotech/GM Crops—2010*. Ithaca, NY: ISAAA.

CHAPTER 5

Cosmetic Regulatory Harmonization in ASEAN—A View from Industry

SIMON YOUNG
MARK CHONG

Executive Summary

The harmonization of policies and standards is critical to achieving effective integration among states in a regional political and economic bloc such as the Association of Southeast Asian Nations (ASEAN). In September 2003, the ASEAN Economic Ministers signed the agreement on the ASEAN Harmonized Cosmetic Regulatory Scheme. The scheme resulted from five years of cooperation between regulators, the ASEAN Secretariat, and industry and aimed to harmonize cosmetic regulations across the region to increase consumer confidence in product safety and reduce technical barriers to trade.

From the start, the cosmetic industry—represented by national industry associations at the local level and by the ASEAN Cosmetic Association—was actively involved as a partner in the harmonization process. It spoke with one voice, contributed expertise and human resources, and acted in an ethical and constructive manner. This unity, commitment, and responsibility helped the industry build a high level of trust with regulators. Clear ownership from the ASEAN political leadership, coordination and support from the ASEAN Secretariat, and the "win–win–win" strategy for consumers, industry, and regulators also helped ensure the success of the harmonization process.

BACKGROUND

Regional integration and regionalism have been two of the most dynamic phenomena in international affairs. Through regional integration, states aim to realize mutual gains by cooperating within a group of self-motivated states. Since the early 1990s, the world has seen intensified efforts to develop and strengthen regional institutions. This development has culminated in the creation of the North American Free Trade Agreement (NAFTA) in North America, the European Union (EU) in Europe, and Mercosur in Latin America. To attain successful regional cohesion, however, the states within a formal regional group have to overcome the collective action problems that are endemic to international cooperation (Yoshimatsu, 2006).

The Asian financial crisis in 1997–8 and the rapid economic growth of China and India have posed ASEAN member states with serious economic and political challenges (Yoshimatsu, 2006). For example, in 2000, China and India exported 32 per cent less than ASEAN; in 2006, they exported 37 per cent more (Petri, 2009). In response to these challenges, the ASEAN member states have sought to pursue deeper integration, which has required them to reduce intraregional tariff structures and harmonize their domestic rules, policies, and standards (Yoshimatsu, 2006). Successful integration could transform ASEAN into a global powerhouse with the world's third-largest economy in terms of population (behind China and India). In addition, it could significantly increase the region's ability to attract global capital and technology and form partnerships with other regional or global economic entities (Petri, 2009).

The harmonization of policies and standards adopted by all the states in the region is critical to achieving effective integration; this is particularly important for trade facilitation and industrial competitiveness. In Europe, for instance, the harmonization of national standards and the adoption of mutual recognition by member states smoothed the process of market integration (Sandholtz and Zysman, 1989; Hufbauer, 1990).

However, unlike the EU, ASEAN members have little interest in wanting ASEAN to become a supranational body with the authority to enforce rules on all states—Southeast Asia remains beholden to sovereignty as the fundamental principle of stability. Regional integration has been complicated by the expansion of ASEAN membership in the late 1990s to include the Indochina countries, which are at a different stage of economic development from the older members (Yoshimatsu, 2006).

Despite these challenges, ASEAN has endeavored to harmonize national standards with international ones and implement mutual recognition agreements[1] through the ASEAN Consultative Committee on Standards and Quality (ACCSQ).[2] In practice, the harmonization of standards consists of aligning national standards with relevant international standards such as those set by the International Organization for Standardization (ISO), International Electrotechnical Commission (IEC), and International Telecommunications Union (ITU) (Yoshimatsu, 2006).

In 1998, ASEAN leaders agreed to harmonize product standards for 20 priority product groups covering 59 international standards—a process that was completed by the end of 2003. In 1999, ASEAN members agreed on additional harmonization for the safety aspects of electrical products and on electromagnetic compatibility (EMC). The 71 safety standards and ten EMC standards were harmonized in 2004 (Yoshimatsu, 2006).

The 1992 agreement by ASEAN leaders to establish the ASEAN Free Trade Area (AFTA) by 2008 represented a milestone in the organization's attempt to promote economic integration. The main mechanism for achieving AFTA would be the Common Effective Preferential Tariff Scheme, which would lower tariffs on manufactured goods and processed agricultural products to between zero and five per cent and eliminate quantitative restrictions as well as other non-tariff barriers (Yoshimatsu, 2006).

In September 2003, the ASEAN Economic Ministers signed the agreement on the ASEAN Harmonized Cosmetic Regulatory Scheme (AHCRS), which aims to harmonize regulations across the region to reduce technical barriers to trade. This was an important milestone in a process that had been ongoing for the previous five years. The AHCRS will be the focus of the rest of this chapter.

STAKEHOLDER LANDSCAPE

Governments are an important stakeholder group for business organizations, as "they represent the ultimate legislative authority of society and establish the rules within which every organization must function" (Mintzberg, 1983, p44). According to W.C. Ashley (1995), government can best add value to corporate strategy when it aligns business goals with policy development.

ASEAN is a geopolitical and economic organization of ten Southeast Asian countries that was formed in 1967 by Indonesia, Malaysia, the Philippines, Singapore, and Thailand. Since then, membership has expanded to include Brunei, Burma (Myanmar), Cambodia, Laos, and Vietnam. ASEAN aims to foster economic growth, social progress, cultural development, peace, and stability of the region and provide opportunities for member countries to discuss differences peacefully (www.asean.org).

ASEAN had two aims in pursuing the harmonization of cosmetic regulations. First, it wanted to reduce and remove non-tariff trade barriers for cosmetic products between ASEAN member countries. By aligning with a set of internationally recognized cosmetic regulatory principles, harmonization would also reduce non-tariff trade barriers between ASEAN and other major trading blocs, thus facilitating export opportunities. Second, it wanted to increase consumer confidence in—and the safety of—cosmetic products. According to Petri (2009): "To be trusted, the ASEAN brand ... will need to be backed by concrete initiatives to adopt standards and by certifications of adherence to standards by reliable research and testing agencies" (p151).

STRATEGIES CONSIDERED

The ASEAN Cosmetic Association, Inc. (ACA) consists of member organizations from different ASEAN countries that represent the cosmetic industry. Some of ACA's aims are to facilitate the harmonization of cosmetic regulations, upgrade the standards of technical competence and scientific expertise in the local industries, and expand the cosmetic trade in ASEAN. Its current members include:

1. Perkosmi (Indonesia)
2. Federation of Malaysian Manufacturers
3. Chamber of the Cosmetic Industry of the Philippines
4. Thailand Cosmetic Manufacturers Association
5. Cosmetic, Toiletry, & Fragrance Association of Singapore

These local associations have very different makeups and represent a broad range in terms of industry size. Despite the absence of a permanent secretariat, the ACA members are characterized by a strong sense of purpose and unity.

In July 1997, ACA requested assistance from the ASEAN Secretariat and the ACCSQ to harmonize cosmetic regulations across the member states. From the start, ASEAN and ACA adopted the same "win-win-win" strategy:

1. Harmonization represents a win for consumers, as consumers can be assured of getting cosmetic products that meet international standards for quality and safety, as well as faster market access for the latest product innovations that meet these standards.
2. Harmonization represents a win for the cosmetic industry, as it will reduce business costs. With a harmonized regulatory scheme, for example, a Malaysia-based cosmetic manufacturer can market its products in any ASEAN

country without the need to understand unfamiliar and diverse nation-specific regulatory processes in those countries. In addition, its products will meet technical standards such as formulation and packaging requirements and Good Manufacturing Practice guidelines. As the ASEAN regulations are loosely based on those of the European Union, it also means that any product manufactured in ASEAN will be marketable anywhere in Europe (perhaps with minor modifications).

3. Harmonization represents a win for the regulators, for the following reasons:
   - The ability to access regulatory decisions—often made on the basis of extensive and expensive scientific reviews—in other parts of the world.
   - The ability to rapidly respond to international regulatory changes by keeping ASEAN regulations in step with those of other major trading blocs.
   - Facilitation of information exchange between ASEAN member states on the interpretation of regulatory issues—thanks to a common regulatory environment and vocabulary.
   - Facilitation of the management of safety and quality issues across borders.
   - Creation of a critical mass of regulatory and scientific experts from all ten countries.
   - Efficiency gains through the sharing of expertise and training between countries.

The "win-win-win" strategy fostered a high level of trust between ASEAN and ACA. Nonetheless, well before the harmonization process had even begun, individual ACA members (that is, the national cosmetic associations) had already established good relationships with their respective national regulatory bodies. Thus, when ACA, the ASEAN Secretariat, and the ACCSQ started working together on the AHCRS, the strong relationships that already existed between industry and government in each country translated quite effortlessly onto the regional forum.

EXECUTION

While a few of the ASEAN member states had previously undertaken individual initiatives to align parts of their national regulatory standards (particularly in terms of ingredient regulations) with international ones, it was only when ACA engaged with the ASEAN Secretariat and the ACCSQ that intraregional harmonization for cosmetics began to take form.

In July 1998, the Cosmetic Product Working Group (CPWG) was set up at the instigation of the ACCSQ. CPWG was a committee of regulators as well as national and regional industry associations—with coordination from the ASEAN Secretariat—that began the task of harmonizing the technical regulation of cosmetic products. CPWG agreed that the aim should be to develop a common regulatory framework based on the same two objectives that were used for the European Cosmetic Products Directive 76/768/EC:

1. Safe cosmetic products for the consumer in ASEAN.
2. Free movement of goods between member states.

It began by collating existing regulations from all ten ASEAN countries and other major trading blocs/markets, and developing an understanding of the different regulatory approaches. Subsequently, CPWG looked for a suitable regulatory model to use and found it in a set of regulatory principles—known as the Florence Principles—which the international cosmetic industry had proposed. All of these principles were embodied in the European Cosmetic Directive. It helped ACA that the European Cosmetic Directive was already an internationally recognized model that was:

1. Politically acceptable to all parties;
2. Scientifically credible;

3. Proven to work in a trading bloc with several languages and alphabets;
4. Open to modification to suit different conditions; and
5. Supported by both industry and regulators.

Another crucial factor was European Commission support. This support came in the form of funding and expertise—first, in explaining how the regulatory model in Europe worked, and then in detailed training of ASEAN regulators in all aspects of implementation (e.g., on product safety assessment and Good Manufacturing Practice). Between 2003 and 2010, the European Commission—through the ASEAN-EU Program for Regional Integration Support—disbursed ten million euros; it will disburse an additional 15 million euros from 2011 to 2013.

In terms of process, CPWG identified three key areas that had to be addressed:

1. **Develop a set of principles to enable the mutual recognition of products approved under existing national regulations.** This would enable the enactment of bilateral and multilateral trade arrangements. The original vision for the process was that mutual recognition could be rapidly set up between some member countries as a quick and easy first step toward harmonization. Rapid progress was indeed made in identifying and agreeing on the parameters and conditions that needed to be met. However, in order to meet these conditions, the vast majority of member states would have to make significant changes to their existing regulations. When faced with the technical, legal, and political workload associated with this process, all the countries (except one) decided instead to invest their energies into preparing for a single, harmonized regulation. Hence, the first phase of the ACHRS did not materialize.
2. **Draft a single ASEAN regulation that could be translated and enacted in all the member states.** This regulation would replace the diverse existing national regulations

and thus effectively remove technical barriers to trade. By taking the European Cosmetic Products Directive as a template for AHCRS, ASEAN avoided duplicating legislative development and gained access to Europe's long experience in the interpretation and implementation of regulations. Nonetheless, some areas required further clarification, either where detailed guidelines were not available from Europe (e.g., control of product claims, cosmetic Good Manufacturing Practice) or where the delegation of interpretation to European member states had resulted in diverse working practices (e.g., post-market product surveillance, pre-market product notification).

3. **Identify the key technical areas that required the development of specific interpretational guidelines to ensure consistent interpretation across member countries.** ASEAN decided that wherever practical, it would develop detailed guidelines to maximize awareness and agreement among participants before implementation. Although this process delayed the formal signing of the agreement, the participants felt this was preferable to having post-signing implementation inconsistencies. A group of lead countries developed proposals for each of these technical areas, which were then ratified by CPWG prior to adoption.

Industry played a key role in the supply of legal and technical expertise and in drafting many of these guidelines. Nonetheless, responsibility for the decision-making process and the ratification of these guidelines and draft regulations rested with officials from the various national regulatory bodies involved in CPWG (that is, industry did not make these decisions).

In September 2003, all ten ASEAN member states signed the AHCRS, which includes the ASEAN Cosmetic Directive—based loosely on the EU Cosmetic Directive—and the Florence Principles. The common technical requirements under the AHCRS provide a common definition for "cosmetic;" listings of permitted preservatives, ultraviolet absorbers, and colorants; as well as a list of ingredients that cannot be used in cosmetics. In addition, it provides labeling requirements along with guidelines on cosmetic manufacturing practice and cosmetic claims.

CPWG was disbanded once the AHCRS had been signed and was replaced by the ASEAN Cosmetic Committee (ACC), which is responsible for implementing and maintaining the AHCRS. The ACC then created the ASEAN Cosmetic Scientific Body to provide cosmetic scientific advice on technical issues.

In January 2008, ASEAN formally launched the AHCRS, with the last country commencing implementation in January 2011. This means that cosmetic products across ASEAN are now formulated using a single palette of ingredients that is very similar to that used in many other markets, including Europe, Latin America, South Africa, and Eastern Europe. It also means that cosmetic products in all ASEAN countries are manufactured according to the same Good Manufacturing Practice standards; these products are notified to each national regulatory body using the same rapid, transparent process. Moreover, products that are developed for one country can be supplied to all ten ASEAN countries, with just minor labeling changes to account for language differences.

KEY LESSONS

1. **Industry (represented by ACA) was actively involved as a partner in the harmonization process from day one.** Moreover, the industry spoke with one voice, supported the contribution of expertise and human resource to the process, and generally did not attempt to use the process for competitive benefit. This unity, commitment, and responsibility helped the industry build a high level of trust with regulators.
2. **Clear ownership from the ASEAN political leaders—through the Senior Economic Officials' Meeting to**

ACCSQ and ACC—was critical to the success of the initiative. ACA would not have been able to achieve harmonization with a bottom-up approach, as individual countries would have pulled out. The ASEAN Secretariat played an important role in coordinating, supporting, and driving the process.

3. **The "win-win-win" strategy fostered a high level of trust between ASEAN and ACA that facilitated the development of an effective regulatory system.** Nonetheless, it helped that individual ACA members (that is, the national cosmetic associations) had already established good relationships with their respective national regulatory bodies well before the harmonization process began.
4. **Perseverance, patience, and compromise were important.** Many of the highly technical issues took considerable time to resolve. This was especially true for those areas where detailed guidelines and consistent practices were not available from Europe (e.g., Good Manufacturing Practice standards and product notification procedures). In Europe, these areas were left largely undefined and individual member states had developed diverse measures to address them. In the ASEAN process, the various parties agreed that a single set of ASEAN guidelines would be developed. This took time, patience, and compromise—between member states and between industry and regulators.
5. **Communication played an important role.** The participants (both regulators and industry) had to play a key role in explaining to, and educating, groups back in the member countries who had a role to play in successful national implementation. These groups included regulators, legislators, politicians, ministry officials, standard-setting bodies, and local industry (including small and medium enterprises). Through the media, industry associations and regulators also played a role in

briefing the public on the harmonization process and its implications for the consumer and local industry.

CONCLUSION

It may have taken ACA 14 years to achieve harmonization, but the consistency harmonization has brought to cosmetic regulation across ASEAN has made it worthwhile. Yet, some challenges remain. In the absence of central control, individual ASEAN states continuously discuss nonaligned interpretations and new regulations to address local issues. In addition, the European Cosmetic Directive is a moving target—ingredient regulations may change several times in a given year as new safety evidence becomes available. Hence, constant vigilance, good communication, and the identification and use of ASEAN forums are needed to ensure continued harmonization.

Notes

1. A mutual recognition agreement is an international agreement by which two or more countries agree to recognize one another's conformity assessments.
2. The ACCSQ was established at the ASEAN Senior Economic Officials' Meeting in 1992 to eliminate technical trade barriers related to standards and conformance. ACCSQ members are the national standards bodies of member states.

References

ASEAN. (2003). *General Information Booklet on ASEAN Harmonized Cosmetic Regulatory Scheme*. Retrieved from http://www.asean.org/19014.htm.

Ashley, W.C. (1995). Anticipatory management: linking public affairs and strategic planning. In: L.B. Dennis (ed.), *Practical Public Affairs in an Age of Change: A Communication Guide for Business, Government, and College*. Lanham, MD: University Press of America, p239–50.

Hufbauer, G.C. (1990). Overview. In: G.C. Hufbauer (ed.), *Europe 1992: An American Perspective*. Washington, DC: Brookings Institution.

Mintzberg, H. (1983). *Power in and Around Organizations*. Englewood Cliffs, NJ: Prentice Hall.

Petri, P.A. (2009). Competitiveness and leverage. In: M.G. Plummer and S.Y. Chia (eds.), *Realizing the ASEAN Economic Community*. Singapore: ISEAS Publishing, p142–63.

Sandholtz, W. and Zysman, J. (1989). 1992: recasting the European bargain. *World Politics,* **42**(1), 95–128.

Yoshimatsu, H. (2006). Collective action problems and regional integration in ASEAN. *Contemporary Southeast Asia*, **28**(1), 115–40.

CHAPTER 6

Building Corporate Reputation through Community Involvement and Strategic Partnerships—Kraft Hope Kitchens in China

FEI CHE
JIN MONTESANO

Executive Summary

This chapter examines the considerations, approaches, and outcomes of a strategic community program initiated by Kraft Foods in China, in partnership with the China Youth Development Foundation. The chapter outlines the local management team's business rationale for investing in such a program and the lessons learned. The authors assert that the establishment of a strategic community platform that is scalable, sustainable, and socially relevant reinforces Kraft Foods' core business strategies in China, namely, to strengthen relationships with key business partners, increase employee engagement through employee volunteerism, and strengthen its corporate reputation and profile in China.

BACKGROUND

Kraft Foods entered the China market in 1984 with two joint ventures for powdered beverages and coffee. In the 1980s, Tang powdered beverages and Maxwell House coffee were two of the most recognized foreign brands among Chinese consumers. For the next 20 years, Kraft Foods China invested in joint ventures with local Chinese companies and completed the acquisition of Nabisco in 2000. At that time, Kraft Foods' business model in China was focused on modern trade in a few cities. The business had not yet achieved scale or a leadership position in any of the categories in which it played.

Kraft Foods' acquisition of Danone's global biscuits portfolio, LU, in 2007 redefined its position in China. The coming together of two former competitors under one roof created scale for growth and a leadership position in the biscuits category. The new Kraft Foods China developed a strategy with a clear focus in biscuits category leadership.

This focus drove robust growth for leading brands such as Oreo and Chips Ahoy! biscuits. Meanwhile, the company strengthened its consumer research and new product development capabilities with the establishment of its Asia Pacific R&D Center in Suzhou, a city that is only 100 kilometers away from Shanghai, where Kraft Foods China's headquarters is located. With breakthrough innovation, award-winning integrated marketing campaigns, and continued expansion in distribution, the company's business has been on a solid trajectory since 2008, with double-digit growth and consecutive market share gains.

In 2010, Kraft Foods acquired Cadbury and established itself as a leader in not only biscuits but also confectionery. Today, Kraft Foods China is a leader in four core categories: biscuits, powdered beverages, coffee, and confectionery. With eight manufacturing sites and more than 200 sales offices across the country, Kraft Foods' brands such as Oreo, Chips Ahoy!, Prince, Tang, Maxwell House, Halls, and Choclairs have become popular household brands among millions of Chinese consumers.

STAKEHOLDER LANDSCAPE

There is a long-standing expression of doing business in China: How do you sell 1.3 billion toothbrushes to 1.3 billion Chinese? By truly listening to and understanding the Chinese consumers—the stakeholders in the local environment who have influence over how a company conducts its business in one of the most exciting markets in the world. It was imperative that Kraft Foods understood its key stakeholders, namely, the government, media, industry opinion leaders, and community groups, including non-governmental organizations (NGOs).

Chinese Consumers

Chinese society has gone through dramatic changes since Deng Xiaoping's open door policy, which was initiated over three decades ago. While the country continues to deliver high GDP growth even during a global economic recession, the values of the society have demonstrated a shifting emphasis from altruism to personal ambition and wealth creation. Younger, lower middle-class workers with upward aspirations and mobility across all sectors form the backbone of Chinese consumers. Their shopping behaviors are characterized by pragmatism and little loyalty to brands (St-Maurice and Wu, 2006; Roper Reports Worldwide, 2006).

Traditionally, China has been an agricultural society. But urbanization over the past decades has quickly changed that landscape. Some estimates suggest that the 1.3 billion Chinese living in the country are divided into an urban population of about 600 million people and a rural population of about 700 million. Other estimates suggest that up to 80 per cent of Chinese still live in rural environments. As urbanization continues to expand, China's urban population will outnumber the rural population in the foreseeable future.

The Government

President Hu Jintao leads the fourth generation of the Chinese Communist Party. His administration is focused on building a

"Harmonious Society" and promoting "Scientific Development" with clear attention to the social welfare of the disadvantaged. In March 2011, the Chinese government released its 12th Five-Year Plan. Key objectives of the plan include rebalancing the economy, ameliorating social inequality, and protecting the environment. Multinational companies are acknowledged as having best practices in the area of advanced management know-how, corporate governance, innovation, and technology. Under the direction of the 12th Five-Year Plan, the Chinese government will raise its expectations for global corporations to lead in areas such as tax and economic contribution, harmonious labor relations, and environmental best practices in China. At the same time, multinational companies that fail to meet the regulations or standards set by the government in these areas are likely to receive a disproportionate amount of scrutiny from the government.

The Media

Today, the most dynamic changes are taking place in Chinese media trends. Not only is there a growing number of news outlets and channels, there is significant fragmentation within media as consumers are spoiled for choice in terms of how and when they can consume the news. China has about 1,938 newspapers, 9,468 periodicals, 2,432 radio stations, and more than 3,108 TV channels. Blogs and other types of online media are on an accelerated growth curve. China's Internet users have exceeded 400 million. There is no doubt that the government still sets the tone for news reporting. However, the thriving business community and the growing middle class have provided an attractive environment for the flourishing of business news, lifestyle magazines, and entertainment programs (General Administration of Press and Publication, 2007).

Even television is flourishing and diversifying. The Chinese population used to receive national and global news and current affairs from one main source: China Central Television (CCTV). Although CCTV still dominates nationwide coverage because of its broad footprint, large municipal TV stations such as Beijing TV and Shanghai TV have become the primary choices for most local residents seeking news and current information. In the city of Guangzhou, Hong Kong TV channels have become the most popular choices for local residents. Some provincial satellite stations, for example, Hunan Satellite TV, are even competing head to head with CCTV for national audiences.

Official media aside, new media is playing an increasingly important role in Chinese lives. Mirroring patterns in many parts of the world, BBS (Bulletin Board Systems), blogs, popular sites such as Kaixin Net, YouTube, and mobile messaging have become key sources of information for the young generation. There are 233 million users surfing the Internet via cell phones, 102 million regular BBS users, and close to 200 million Chinese bloggers. Because of new media, people no longer need to rely on state media for news and information. For any major event or development, people are turning more and more to the Internet and then voicing their opinions about what is going on (China Internet Network Information Center, 2009).

Nongovernmental Organizations and Special Interest Groups

NGOs in China used to have strong government roots and carried out projects more or less according to the prescribed government approach. In recent years, grassroots volunteerism has begun to play an increasingly important role in disaster relief and environment protection. NGOs will be able to play a more active role in Chinese society with further relaxing of regulations and the lowering of registration thresholds. That said, the variety and sheer number of NGOs operating in China today provides corporations with a much broader range of potential partners to engage in social and community issues.

Given the political and social structure of China today, companies that seek to build a community project that will succeed at the grassroots level—covering a vast geographical footprint and reaching a broad cross-section of beneficiaries—must secure the endorsement and support of local government at the county, municipal, and sometimes provincial levels. Working with an NGO partner that has an existing network and track record of securing the support of various levels of local government will enable companies to achieve their community or CSR objectives.

STRATEGIES AND EXECUTION

Kraft Foods began to leverage its newfound scale and grow strongly in 2008. The management team realized that its need to compete for the best talent in the market was hampered by the company's relatively low profile in the market. Many foreign companies have invested aggressively to establish their profiles in China over the past three decades. Kraft Foods found that it did not enjoy a strong reputation or level of visibility to match its commercial position. It therefore made a decision to create a strategic, scalable, and locally relevant community program that would underscore the company's long-term commitment to the country and provide its talent with a clearer definition of what Kraft Foods would stand for in Chinese society. A key factor of success in this important market would be in establishing strong relationships with the company's key business partners. The management team believed that investing in the right strategic community partnership program would reinforce the business's core strategy for growth. Not only would such a program anchor the company as a "resident" and not just a "visitor" in China, but if well executed it would also serve as a powerful way to strengthen employee engagement and strengthen relationships with key business partners.

Internal assessments conducted by Kraft Foods led the team to consider programs tackling hunger and malnutrition in rural schools. Most of the students attending rural schools were children left behind in the villages by their migrant worker parents who lived and worked in coastal cities. As a result, schools and grandparents looked after the children's nutrition and food supply, often without much resource or knowledge. After carefully screening through the NGO candidates with experience in rural children's education and growth, Kraft Foods China decided to reach out to the China Youth Development Foundation (CYDF), one of the leading charity organizations in China. CYDF is well known internationally for building more than 16,000 Project Hope rural schools in the poorest regions of China since the 1980s. Many leading multinational and Chinese companies have partnered with CYDF to build Project Hope schools. The Kraft Foods China Corporate Affairs team began a dialogue with CYDF about the state of hunger and malnutrition in the country, root causes, and strategies for tackling the issue. In May 2009, Kraft Foods China and CYDF commissioned independent research to better understand the scope and extent of hunger and malnutrition in rural schoolchildren. A total of 106 rural primary schools in 17 provinces participated in the survey, and stakeholders—from the headmasters of each school to kitchen staff and primary schoolchildren—were interviewed about their meals, hygiene practices, and nutritional knowledge.

The findings of the report were highly informative. The report underscored three critical areas of need among surveyed rural primary schools: Hunger and nutrition deficiency among students between the ages of six and 12 was common. Almost no schools had canteen facilities that met national food hygiene standards; and where they existed, food safety, sanitation, and hygiene standards were low. Lack of understanding of nutrition also hampered school teachers, administrators, and students. The majority of students did not have the opportunity to consume meat even on a weekly basis. Nearly 70 per cent of students experienced hunger during classes, and more than 30 per cent of surveyed students did not get enough food. Only half of all schools surveyed were equipped with some canteen facilities, but these were found to be inadequate; of those, 30 per cent were able only to heat food brought by students and did not offer cooked meals. None of the surveyed schools were equipped with basic kitchen equipment needed for cleaning, sterilizing, washing, storing, freezing, and processing food. More than 50 per cent of schools surveyed did not have the capacity to provide clean and sanitary drinking water to students. Fifty-two per cent of teachers said students occasionally became ill because of poor food hygiene. Canteen food suppliers could not provide food hygiene quarantine certificates.

CYDF and Kraft Foods identified the schools that would be appropriate beneficiaries of the Kraft Hope Kitchen project. Clear metrics for the program were agreed upon, both quantitative and qualitative. Quantitative measures included number of kitchens built, number and types of equipment required to set up a Kraft Hope Kitchen, training programs for school headmasters, food donation mechanisms, and volunteer services contributed after the kitchens were built. Qualitative metrics included regular feedback from students, teachers, and volunteers. CYDF and Kraft Foods employees formed a Quality Review Committee that would be responsible for checking, reviewing, and approving the construction of all kitchens to agreed specifications. The key elements of a Kraft Hope Kitchen were straightforward—floors, walls, ceilings, pest-resistant facilities, refrigeration, disinfection cabinets, chopping boards, storage rooms, student hand sinks, dining tables, and chairs—all to agreed standards and specifications.

Source: Courtesy of Kraft Foods China Corporate & Government Affairs

On 15 October 2009, Kraft Foods and CYDF launched their first school kitchen in Shucheng County, Anhui province. Together, the partners announced plans to build 100 Kraft Hope Kitchens in 100 primary schools across five provinces—Anhui, Yunan, Jilin, Hunan, and Hebei. The Miachong Project Hope School in Shucheng County was the first recipient of a Kraft Hope Kitchen. Wang Min, Deputy Secretary General of CYDF, Anhui provincial and Shucheng County government officials, and 70 employee volunteers from Kraft Foods China—including its then President, Lorna Davis—were present to witness the completion of the first Kraft Hope Kitchen. From January to June 2010, the Quality Review Committee worked to assess and approve the construction of a further 99 kitchens in five provinces until they were fully operational.

A core deliverable of the program was to build professional-grade school kitchens with canteens, but the educational component of the partnership was also an important factor for its success. The CYDF and Kraft Foods' program aimed to improve food safety and hygiene as well as nutrition education in schools and among the school community. Nutrition education materials and collaterals such as posters, booklets, and teaching aids were developed to help teachers and kitchen staff understand the basic food groups and their roles in a nutritionally balanced diet. Kraft Foods developed visual aids to support understanding of the nutrition and food safety guidance issued by the China Nutrition Society that is available to all citizens. These student education materials were developed with fun, easy-to-read language and graphics that were age appropriate, and students were encouraged to share these learning tips at home with their parents and grandparents.

The support of business partners was an important contribution to the expansion of Kraft Hope Kitchens. Inspired by the program's progress and impact, business partners donated an additional US$143,000 to CYDF to expand the program's aims by building more kitchens in 2011. Aside from cash donation, some partners—such as Yi Hai Kerry Group—also donated nutritious food products, such

Source: Courtesy of Kraft Foods China Corporate & Government Affairs

as soy milk powder, to Kraft Hope Kitchen schools. Yao Ming, the basketball legend and a national hero, was the ambassador for Kraft Foods' Oreo's "Twist, Lick, but Can You Dunk?" campaign in 2010. As founder of the Yao Ming Foundation, Yao showed tremendous support for the Kraft Hope Kitchens program, not only inviting CYDF and Kraft Foods to build school kitchens in the rural schools built by his own foundation, but also by donating autographed T-shirts and basketballs for Kraft Hope Kitchen's fund-raising efforts.

The Kraft Hope Kitchen Volunteer Committee was established in December 2009 by employee volunteers. The committee came together organically, to the pleasant surprise of both the President of Kraft Foods China and the Corporate Affairs team, which was the function responsible for developing and leading this project. As with all corporate community programs, employee volunteerism is a critical component. Rather than waiting to be organized into groups, Kraft Foods employees were so inspired by the program's concept and filled with pride by the business's decision to invest in this program that they proactively volunteered to organize an internal committee that would support and facilitate the program's execution through a dependable and continuous supply of employee volunteers to work with CYDF, school administrators, vendors, suppliers, and business partners. The committee even chose its own vision: "Kraft Hope Kitchens—a delicious way to provide healthy nutrition to children." Since the program was launched, the Kraft Hope Kitchen Volunteer Committee has contributed over 2,800 volunteer hours, with a registered employee volunteer base of more than 320 employees. The committee has organized employee volunteers to participate in new Kraft Hope Kitchen site selection in partnership with CYDF, as well as to host a day of fun activities

BEFORE: **AFTER:**

Source: Courtesy of Kraft Foods China Corporate & Government Affairs

including sports, recreation, and nutrition education for students in the newly opened kitchen.

In 2011, additional donations from business partners and Kraft Foods China employees are enabling CYDF and Kraft Foods to build 50 new kitchens in rural provinces that have not yet benefited from this program. For instance, CYDF and Kraft Foods built ten new kitchens in May and June 2011 in Le Du County, Qinghai province.

At the time of writing, over 110 Kraft Hope Kitchens were in full operation. More are being built with continued donations from those interested in seeing this program continue. Current kitchens in operation benefit 60,000 rural schoolchildren across six provinces. These kitchens serve hot nutritious meals prepared by trained cooks under good hygiene and sanitary standards. For many of these primary schoolchildren, this is the most nutritionally important meal of the day. Throughout the development and execution of this program, CYDF and Kraft Foods have educated key external stakeholders about the program, its aims, and its progress. Not only did the two partners drive external communications and outreach, but at every milestone they engaged local and provincial government officials, party leaders, and media whose support and contributions would be critical to the success of this program.

The management team at Kraft Foods also played their part: ever vigilant about promoting the flagship CSR program, team members would share a standard narrative on Kraft Hope Kitchen whenever they had the opportunity to present the company for the first time at various speaking engagements and external meetings. Human Resources would talk about the Kraft Hope Kitchen program to potential new candidates at recruitment fairs, at universities, and to executive search firms. Marketing has plans to roll out the Kraft Hope Kitchen logo and information on some product packaging. Corporate Affairs set up and maintains a dedicated Kraft Hope Kitchen website to raise awareness and expand the program to more interested parties: www.krafthopekitchen.com.

The program has gained some notable recognition. In November 2010, the Kraft Hope Kitchen program with CYDF received the American Chamber of Commerce's Corporate Social Responsibility Award. In April 2011, the program won a Rotary Leadership Award for Building Community in China.

In a separate exercise, Kraft Foods Asia Pacific's Corporate Affairs commissioned an external consultancy to conduct a regional corporate reputation stakeholder audit. This is a key element in the regional strategy for the Corporate Affairs function in Asia Pacific. The survey found that Kraft Foods' corporate reputation in China exceeded that of leading global fast moving consumer goods companies and home-grown food and beverage industry peers, with 49 per cent of survey respondents saying Kraft Foods' reputation in China was "excellent" and 39 per cent saying it was "good." Kraft Foods China had the highest reputation score across surveyed markets. In the important area of *stakeholder expectations*, survey respondents were asked to score their expectation of a leading food and beverage company regarding certain attributes, such as "leading in the area of community and social responsibility." Kraft Foods China not only met but exceeded stakeholder expectations in this category. Analysis of these metrics suggested that the Kraft Hope Kitchen program was the "thin edge of the wedge," cutting through the clutter to shape and strengthen Kraft Foods' reputation in this market. Not only were business partners, government officials, media, and employees more aware of Kraft Foods' engagement in the community through this program, more consumers were becoming more aware about the program through consistent and well-told external communications and media outreach.

Kraft Hope Kitchen remains at the early stages of its evolution, and as a result many lessons are yet to be learned from this new partnership. The strong start is encouraging, however, for CYDF, Kraft Foods employees, and Kraft Foods' business partners who are excited by the prospect of expanding on this program in the future.

LESSONS LEARNED

1. **A strategic CSR platform is one that both reinforces the core strategy of the business and addresses a compelling local social need.** A process for identifying such a program begins with an external review and analysis of risks and opportunities, and an alignment process with internal stakeholders.
2. **Enable employees to own the program early to build lasting momentum for the program.** A key aspect of this program's runaway success has been the early and proactive interest of employees in being part and parcel of this program's management and execution. With the management support of the Kraft Hope Kitchen Volunteer Committee, the organic employee volunteer unit offers employees a chance to become part of the co-creation early in the program. Employees at all levels developed a strong sense of ownership of the program concept, which gave them the opportunity to be part of something much bigger than their day jobs, and to develop a sense of pride and contribution to community that went beyond their normal responsibilities.
3. **Communicate early and frequently, and leverage a wide net of champions.** Despite the complexity of the program, the partners invested in a communications strategy that engaged the media, business partners, and other relevant stakeholders at every milestone. The low but steady drumbeat of news on the program, over time, developed a momentum of its own.

CONCLUSION

Corporate Social Responsibility programs come in all shapes and sizes to address a host of business objectives. In Kraft Foods' case, it looked to a strategic program to increase employee engagement, improve its corporate reputation, and strengthen relationships with key business partners. Not only were business partners, government stakeholders, and employees more aware of Kraft Foods' engagement in the community through this program, more consumers were becoming more aware about the program through consistent and well-told external communications and media outreach. The Kraft Hope Kitchen program remains at the early stages of its evolution, and as a result many lessons are yet to be learned from this new partnership. The strong start is encouraging. The CYDF, Kraft Foods, and the latter's business partners are excited by the prospect of expanding this program in the future.

References

China Internet Network Information Center. *Twenty-fourth Statistical Report on Internet Development in China 2009.* Retrieved from http://www1.cnnic.cn/uploadfiles/pdf/2009/10/12/114121.pdf.

General Administration of Press and Publication. *National Press and Publication Statistics 2007.* Retrieved from http://www.gapp.gov.cn/cms/html/21/490/200808/459129.html.

Roper Reports Worldwide, 2006.

St-Maurice, I. and Wu, C. (2006). Understanding China's teen consumers. *McKinsey Quarterly (Special Edition: Serving the New Chinese Consumer)*, 52–9. Retrieved from http://mkqpreview2.qdweb.net/PDF-Download.aspx?ar = 1797.

CHAPTER 7

Infusing Corporate Values and Delivering Brand Promise—Singapore Airlines' Experience

MARK CHONG

Executive Summary

This chapter examines the internal communication and training functions at Singapore Airlines—one of the world's best international airlines—and how they are used strategically to enable cabin crew and ground staff to live the company's corporate values and consistently deliver on its brand promise of being "a great way to fly." It shows that internal communication and training should be treated as the "first frontier" in the battle for the customer: when it is founded on strong corporate values, internal communication and training can help transform key employees such as cabin crew into "walking embodiments" of the core values, and key touch points into opportunities for fulfilling the brand promise.

BACKGROUND[1]

Launched in 1972, Singapore Airlines (SIA) is a globally renowned brand and one of the most profitable airlines in the world. Its world-class service, innovative offerings, and modern fleet have won the company numerous international accolades over the years. In 2010, *Business Traveler US* voted SIA Best Overall Airline in the World for the 20th time. In the same year, SIA was ranked one of the world's 50 most admired companies (ranked 27th) by *Fortune* magazine.

Over the past 20 years, SIA has been synonymous with innovation and world-class service. The company has had a history of "firsts;" for example, it was the first commercial airline in the world to fly nonstop from London to Singapore (1989), to introduce a satellite-based in-flight telephone service (1991), to offer audio- and video-on-demand capabilities in its in-flight entertainment systems (1997), to bring together a comprehensive panel of world-renowned chefs to develop in-flight meals (2001), and to operate the world's longest nonstop commercial flights—between Singapore and Los Angeles and between Singapore and New York (2004). In 2007, it became the world's first airline to fly the Airbus A380. Its commitment to cultivating and delivering world-class service is manifested in its commitment to cabin and ground crew training.

SIA's core promise focuses on the in-flight experience—the personal service and service-related comforts—which is embodied by the airline's now famous *sarong kebaya*-clad stewardesses. Thanks to a highly successful branding campaign, the SIA stewardess has become an international icon known affectionately as "the Singapore Girl." The Singapore Girl is the essence of SIA's unique style of service. She "mirrors her Asian heritage—natural femininity, natural grace and warmth, and a natural, gentle way with people" (Batey, 2002, p120). To ensure that customers get the best in-flight experience, SIA has also pioneered a number of service "firsts" in the airline industry, including offering "the largest drink menu in the skies, the largest complement of cabin crew, and the most comfortable seats" (Batey, 2002, p136).

THE STAKEHOLDER LANDSCAPE: EMPLOYEES AND INTERNAL COMMUNICATION

There has been considerable focus on how external communication—such as advertising and public relations—helps corporations build a corporate image to differentiate themselves from competitors in an increasingly crowded marketplace. This corporate image is important as it is a basis on which stakeholders choose to establish contact or business transactions with the organization and whether or not to attach good or ill will toward it (Schuler, 2004). However, the role of internal communication and training in building corporate brands has received less attention in the literature.

Internal communication merits close attention as employees may be the most important audience for a company's organizational communication and corporate branding efforts (Christensen and Askegaard, 2001). Indeed, employees are considered one of the most trusted information sources about an organization (Dortok, 2006). This is because they embody the corporate brand, and interactions between them and external stakeholders communicate the brand's values as much as (if not more than) traditional marketing communication (de Chernatony, 2002). Perhaps nowhere is this more important than in service industries, where employees are routinely the contact point between a company's internal and external environments and where the interactions or "moments of truth" (Gummeson, 1999) can deliver the brand promise and create a powerful image and experience among customers through appropriate behavior—or not (Hardaker and Fill, 2005). Hence, service companies need to instill shared understandings of their brand values in the hearts and minds of employees to enhance brand-supporting behaviors (Vallaster and de Chernatony, 2005).

Employees who are aligned with the company's values can help their organization attain a sustainable competitive advantage by giving external stakeholders experiences of these values. Thus, "employees represent significant brand value and an organization's leadership has a responsibility to marshal this opportunity" (Hardaker and Fill, 2005, p375). Nonetheless, it is not good enough that employees understand the company's brand values and have the right skills if the goal is to have "brand ambassadors:" they also have to believe in and internalize the brand values through the enactment of appropriate behaviors (Vallaster and de Chernatony, 2005).

Effective corporate branding requires all company employees to adopt and behave according to a company's set of core values (Collins and Porras, 2002; Harris and de Chernatony, 2001). Thus, strong corporate brands are associated with employees who are closely aligned with the core corporate values (Ackerman, 2000). Values[2] are especially important as they are at the core of the corporate brand, are critical to how service brands differentiate themselves, and can inspire behavioral changes, motivation, and commitment (Durgee *et al.*, 1996; Jones, 1999; Schultz *et al.*, 2000). For example, values can guide how an organization and its employees deal with the uncertainty that is inherent in uncontrollable or difficult events (Schein, 1992).

The synergy between corporate values, employees' effective enactment of these values, and customers' appreciation of them is critical to the success of a corporate brand. In fact, it is precisely the interactions between the value-providing behavior of a company's employees and the value-seeking behavior of customers that sustain ongoing communication between internal and external shareholders (de Chernatony and Dall'Olmo Riley, 1999; de Chernatony, 2002). When employees understand and are aligned with the core values, they have a better appreciation of their roles and higher commitment to delivering the brand promise, resulting in higher brand performance. Thus, shared values have been shown to explain employees' customer-directed service behaviors that go beyond their formal job descriptions or role requirements (Bettencourt and Brown, 1997; Maxham and Netemeyer, 2003). Conversely, it would be considerably more difficult for employees to enact a company's core values if there was a misalignment between the corporation's and employees' values (Heskett, 1987; Kotter and Heskett, 1992; de Chernatony, 2002).

Nonetheless, if values are not internalized it may mean that employees will say one thing in a given situation and actually do something quite different altogether. As employees inadvertently communicate corporate values through their behavior (Kennedy, 1977; Post and Griffin, 1997; Saxton, 1998), organizations need to help employees internalize the organization's core values in their attitudes and behavior through communication, training, and the allocation of rewards and punishment (Ashforth and Mael, 1989; Schein, 1992; Stuart, 1999; de Chernatony, 1999; Andriopoulos and Gotsi, 2001).

As companies "increasingly compete based on their ability to express who they are and what they stand for" (Schultz *et al.*, 2000, p80), service brands need to depend on internal communication to empower employees to deliver on the brand promise (Camp, 1996; Cleaver, 1999; Hardaker and Fill, 2005). If employees understand the company's goals and their own role in achieving them, they are more likely to want—and to be able to support—these goals in their interactions with external stakeholders (Zyman, 2002). Companies that attach higher importance to internal communication (such as setting up a separate internal communication department) are known to have higher levels of employee engagement (Thomson and Hecker, 2000) and better reputations (Dortok, 2006).

Nonetheless, internal communication must be a two-way affair, as "successful corporate brands are characterized by participative approaches whereby senior management provide guidance about their core values, but find mechanisms to engage staff in discussions about their values to encourage a mediated, consensus view" (de Chernatony, 2002, p119). It is simply insufficient for a company to write down its vision and values and hope that employees will "live" them. Instead, the company must engage its employees in a dialogue about what the vision and values mean to them if it hopes to have the vision and values internalized by employees (Bennis, 1997). This is borne out in a Gallup survey that showed that employee disengagement was related to a lack of communication with management (Liang, 2006).

Perhaps never have employees played a more critical role in organizational success than in an "experience economy." In such an economy, the consumer is a "guest" who is looking for a highly personal and memorable contact with the brand. Thus, creating indelible impressions—the "takeaways" of the experience—on customers with positive cues is of paramount importance (Pine and Gilmore, 1998).

Brand values play a critical role in this "experience economy" because they drive employee behavior, and "values enacted by employees notably determine the success of the service encounter in the eyes of the consumer" (de Chernatony and Drury, 2004, p75). On their part, consumers are generally attracted to service brands that are perceived as having values congruent to their own, and this gravitation occurs primarily through the value-enacting behavior of customer-facing employees (Wilson, 2001; Davies and Chun, 2002; de Chernatony and Drury, 2004).

The potential variability and highly personal nature of service brand offerings makes it critical for organizations to align staff behavior with core brand values (LePla and Parker, 1999). Internal communication and training perform this alignment by fostering the internalization of brand values by employees, which bolsters their commitment to enact brand-supporting behaviors (Thomson *et al.*, 1999). In turn, these brand-supporting behaviors—when performed consistently over a period of time—ensure that customers (or guests) have the most personal and memorable experience of the brand's promise.

STRATEGIES AND EXECUTION

Internal Communication

SIA's employee communication program is based on the mission and key corporate values of the company. SIA's mission is to be "a global company dedicated to providing air transportation services of the highest quality and to maximizing returns for the benefit of its shareholders and employees." Its core corporate values are the pursuit of excellence, safety, customer first, concern for staff, integrity, and teamwork.

SIA Group had 21,534 employees worldwide (as of 31 March 2011). Of these, cabin crew members make up the single largest group. The rest of the employees comprise overseas staff, pilots, managers, administrative officers, and "rank and file" staff. The 7,304 cabin crew members and 2,335 pilots (as of 31 March 2011) represent an internal communication challenge as they are always "on the move" and almost never in one place altogether at the same time.

The number of communication tools at SIA is impressive for its comprehensiveness and specificity. Print publications such as *Outlook* are supplemented with more timely electronic bulletin boards and e-mail updates. Moreover, the company has channels that are tailored to the specific communication needs of its very important cabin crew and pilots. For example, the Cabin Crew Division produces three publications specifically for the cabin crew. *Highpoint* is a monthly newsletter that features cabin crew events and passenger comments. *Cabin Crew Circulars* are biweekly updates on service procedures, rules and regulations, security, and safety guidelines. In addition, the division sends out electronic news online through a cabin crew online portal and mass e-mail updates for urgent announcements. There are also preflight briefings conducted by in-flight supervisors or the chief steward/stewardess as well as cabin crew business meetings and fleet meetings for pilots.

Nonetheless, what makes SIA stand out is the number of face-to-face communication channels. Meetings and road shows enable employees to engage with management directly and are tailored to the communication needs of different employee groups. *In Sync* is a fortnightly "meet the people" session in which the Senior Vice President of the Cabin Crew Division meets cabin crew on an informal basis; anyone can talk about anything in freewheeling and open-ended sessions. Then, there are dialogue sessions and ward get-togethers that allow cabin crew and management to address specific issues and express their views in face-to-face settings. In addition, road shows give senior management the opportunity to communicate key issues and new initiatives directly and to obtain feedback from the ground. SIA also conducts focus groups: these are agenda-driven and focus on generating cabin crew insights on topics such as organizational climate. According to Mitchell (2002, p102): "There's no substitute for personal contact from the organization's highest levels." It is significant that union members are involved in all meetings and training sessions—their involvement helps to break down walls between unions and management and inculcate a sense of ownership. At SIA, it seems there is no such thing as "overcommunication."

Lastly, SIA administers the organizational climate survey to all the employees working in its Singapore headquarters. The first voluntary organizational climate survey conducted in August/September 2005 yielded a response rate of 57 per cent. Survey results are communicated through several communication channels. Significantly, the results are factored into the performance assessment of the company's heads of department. SIA aims to conduct the survey every two years to benchmark progress in key performance areas, including communication. The communication emphasis is important, as "making communication an integral part of any performance review will guarantee that this value permeates all levels of an organization" (Argenti and Forman, 2002, p144).

Infusing Corporate Values

SIA's relentless communication of its core values reflects its strategic status in the company's internal communication and training programs. Accordingly, the company's six core values are communicated to all employees at four different "touch points" in their tenure—when they first join the company, when they attend training programs, when they attend corporate events, and through corporate communication channels such as *Outlook*.

When non-cabin crew employees first join SIA, they undergo an induction program that includes a segment on the company's core values. In addition to showing new employees the SIA core values video, the trainers use actual cases to explain what it means to adopt the core values at the workplace, thus showing how these values can help employees to convey and live the brand promise. Core values are also reiterated during ongoing training programs, such as the New Managers' Program for newly promoted managers and team-building courses. The company's senior managers (including the Chairman and CEO) also harp on the importance of living the core values when they speak at major events such as the Long Service Awards ceremony and other company functions. According to Cheney (1983), senior executives play a crucial role in influencing and persuading employees to identify with the corporation and develop a distinctive corporate identity. The core values are also printed in each issue of *Outlook* magazine, and each employee is given a pocket-sized copy of the core value statements.

By incorporating these core values into employees' key touch points, SIA aims—over time—to infuse them into employees to the extent that they "live" these values. And when they do, "customers are much more likely to experience the company in a way that's consistent with what you've promised" (Mitchell, 2002, p100).

SIA has an evaluation system in place to ensure that core values are aligned with behavior. In fact, demonstration of behavioral alignment with the company's core values is one of the performance indicators in every employee's annual performance appraisal. When there are shortfalls, the supervisor (in consultation with the employee) will recommend remedial activities or provide additional supervision. The performance of crew members is measured using an on-board assessment (OBA) that is carried out by a more senior crew member on the same flight. Significantly, the OBA incorporates performance indicators that reflect the company's core values, such as service orientation and product knowledge (pursuit of excellence), safety and security (safety), and work relationships and people management (teamwork) (Heracleous *et al.*, 2006). The OBA is reinforced by a strong sense of collective destiny that developed historically from SIA's early days, when its employees knew that the Singapore state—its majority owner—would not subsidize the airline to keep it financially viable. The company's evaluation and reward system sustains this feeling by fostering peer pressure to perform (Heracleous *et al.*, 2006).

Cabin Crew: The Crucial "Touch Point"

SIA's cabin crew is undoubtedly the critical touch point between the organization and its passengers. Thus, cabin crew members attend the airline industry's longest basic training program—four months—to ensure that they embody SIA's corporate values and realize the promise of being "A Great Way to Fly." This training focuses not only on functional skills, but also on "soft" skills such as intercultural communication, personal poise, and negotiation skills involved in dealing with demanding passengers (Davis, 1996). Nonetheless, new cabin crew members are invited to join the company only after undergoing a rigorous three-stage interview process that weeds out candidates whose personal values are divergent from the company's. Indeed, employees who "share an organization's values are more likely to feel like an integral part of the system, taking ownership in and responsibility for the firm and its performance" (Maxham and Netemeyer, 2003, p58). Once employees join SIA, the training serves to enhance alignment between the cabin crew's personal value system and SIA's corporate values.

From the start, trainees are expected to start manifesting these values—such as greeting and making eye contact with everyone they come into contact with—so that they gradually, but surely, become the "Singapore Girl" that they aspire to be. In short, cabin crew members are groomed to be "walking" embodiments and manifestations of these core values. For example, one of the core corporate values is "Customer First." Thus, cabin crew members are expected to put on a smile and take care of their passengers even when they are under duress. "Pursuit of excellence" is another core value that is manifested in the impeccable poise and service of the cabin crew.

To attune cabin crew to the cultural characteristics and sensitivities (e.g., taboos) of their multinational market, SIA gets experienced international crew members to impart in training programs their knowledge of the verbal and behavioral subtleties exhibited by their own cultures. In addition, SIA offers free language-and-culture classes aimed at enhancing crews' understanding of their passengers.

Training does not stop after the four-month immersion program—it goes on for the entire term of employment. These programs continually reinforce the alignment of personal with corporate values through the communication and sharing of core value-affirming experiences. After all, "identification is not a one-time, all or nothing process whereby individuals come to match their values with their organization. It is an ongoing process that requires adequate management attention" (Andriopoulos and Gotsi, 2001, p153).

SOAR—"Service Over and Above the Rest"—is a good example of the above philosophy. Launched in 2003, the training program aims to realize SIA's mission of providing in-flight service that far exceeds the competition. SOAR inculcates a unique set of values that are aligned with the core values but which are articulated in a form that resonates best with cabin crew. For example, the SOAR value of "A passenger's smile makes it all worthwhile" is linked to the core value of "Customer First." So, despite the existence of core values, companies sometimes find it necessary to have customized messages or distinctive employee value propositions for different employee subsegments (Martin and Hetrick, 2006). A typical SOAR session is based on the sharing of scenarios and situations actually encountered by other cabin crew in the past. This sharing intensifies the learning and bonding between participants as they come to a common understanding of the SOAR values and their enactment in a wide variety of circumstances. The training derives much of its credibility and immediacy from the fact that it is often conducted by senior cabin crew members who have personally experienced those situations.

The degree of attention to communication in SOAR is nothing short of impressive. A one-day session that the author attended featured modules on interpersonal and intercultural communication skills. In the interpersonal communication module, for example, the topic of body language alone covered facial expression, eye movement, posture, gestures, personal space, breathing, and appearance. The subtopic of posture was a mini-lesson in and of itself: trainees learned (among other things) to always position themselves perpendicularly and bend forward when speaking with a passenger—these "postures" communicate the avoidance of confrontation and the eagerness to serve, respectively. SIA cabin crew trainees the author spoke to described their four-month training stint as "grueling," but reported positive transformations in their attitudes toward people and service.

Nonetheless, cabin crew can only manifest their core and SOAR values to the extent that their internal stakeholders allow them to—misunderstanding, miscommunication, or a lack of cooperation from ground and engineering staff can potentially derail their best efforts. SIA's *Fus3ion* course aims precisely to enhance cooperation among pilots, cabin crew, ground staff, and engineering staff. For example, *Fus3ion* features a role-play program that gets pilots to "act" as ground staff, ground staff to "act" as engineers, engineers to "act" as cabin crew, and cabin crew to "act" as pilots. This exercise develops empathy and patience by putting individuals in the shoes of their colleagues. As frontline employees (e.g., ticketing officers and station managers) also play a significant role in manifesting the company's core values, they undergo an equivalent training program known as "Transforming Customer Service."

By ensuring that both crew and non-crew employees share similar understandings of the core values, SIA makes consistent brand-supporting behavior possible across different customer "touch points" (Mohammed and Ringseis, 2001; Vallaster and de Chernatony, 2005). Indeed, non-crew members' understanding of SIA's core values is borne out by the company's Organizational Climate Surveys.

In summary, SIA's core values form the bedrock of its internal communication and training programs, which work in mutually reinforcing ways to internalize these values in cabin crew and other employees to empower them to deliver on SIA's brand promise of "A Great Way to Fly."

G. Soenon and B. Moingeon's (2002) multifaceted model of corporate identity offers a holistic way of showing how internal communication and training contribute to the alignment of different aspects of SIA's identity. These five facets are:

1. **Professed identity.** It refers to "what a group or organization professes about itself" (Soenen and Moingeon, 2002, p18). Nonetheless, researchers often study the *professed identity* only when it is projected toward specific audiences through various communications (that is, when it becomes the *projected identity*).
2. **Projected identity.** It refers to "the elements an organization uses, in more or less controlled ways, to present itself to specific audiences" (Soenen and Moingeon, 2002, p18). Perhaps the most visible and well-known aspect of SIA's *projected identity* for external audiences is the image of the Singapore Girl. As mentioned earlier, the Singapore Girl is the essence of SIA's unique style of service. Another prominent aspect of the company's externally *projected identity* is its positioning as an innovative airline that offers passengers the latest and best in in-flight services. Internally, its *projected identity* is enshrined in its six core values, which are conveyed and reinforced through internal communication and training programs.
3. **Experienced identity.** It refers to "what organizational members experience, more or less consciously, with regard to their organization" (Soenen and Moingeon, 2002, p19).
4. **Manifested identity.** It refers to an organization's "historical identity" or "elements that have characterized

the organization over a period of time" (Soenen and Moingeon, 2002, p20). Over the past 20 years, SIA has displayed innovation and world-class service, as detailed above.

5. **Attributed identity.** It refers to "attributes that are ascribed to the organization by its various audiences" (Soenen and Moingeon, 2002, p20), and is reflected in the many international accolades heaped on the company.

SIA's *projected identity* is an outcome of its internal communication and training—publications such as the *Outlook* newsletter and training programs such as SOAR formally communicate and reinforce the company's core values. When employees internalize core values and consistently project them in the form of brand-supporting behaviors over a period of time, the *projected identity* becomes *manifested identity*. Brand promise may be said to be delivered when *manifested identity* is expressed consistently over a period of time. *Attributed identity* is formed when external parties confer awards and other accolades on SIA's *manifested identity*. Based on the large number of awards SIA has consistently won over the years for excellence in service and innovation, one can infer that SIA's customers have an extremely positive perception of its service offerings. These awards show that internal communication and training have translated into the delivery of its brand promise of "A Great Way to Fly." Thus, there is a relationship between internal communication and the delivery of brand promise. SIA feeds this *attributed identity* back to its employees through internal communication vehicles and training programs, thus reinforcing employees' *experienced identity*. Aspects of this *experienced identity* in turn feed into SIA's *projected identity*, for example, when employees share their personal experience of the core values in the training sessions and internal publications. Graphically, the four facets form a feedback loop—with internal communication and training programs providing the crucial conduit—which is shown below:

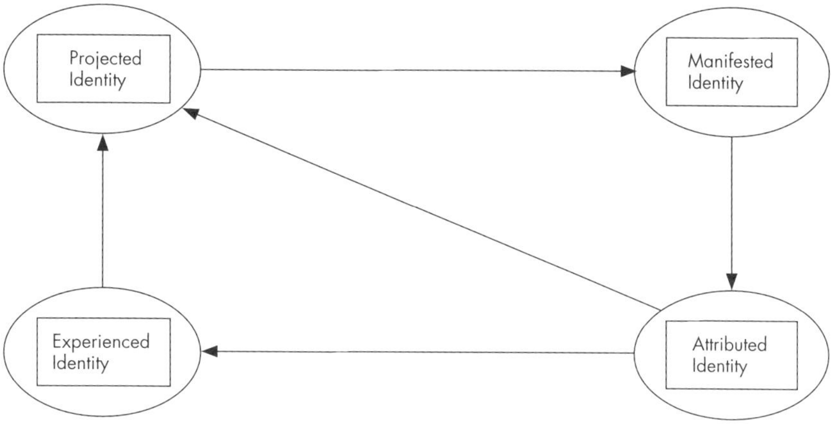

KEY LESSONS

This chapter has shown how internal communication and training enable SIA to consistently deliver on its brand promise to become the world's most successful international airline. Unlike most studies to date, which have focused on the influence of external communication on the corporate image and brand, this chapter shows the strategic role internal communication can play in an organization—especially when it is founded on the organization's core values and intertwined with a training program that borders on zealotry.

What distinguishes SIA's internal communication is its focus on face-to-face dialogue between management and staff as well as communication channels that are tailored to the needs of specific internal stakeholders (e.g., cabin crew). In addition, it is dedicated to the goal of infusing employees—particularly its important cabin crew—with the core values through regular training programs so that they become "walking" and "living" embodiments of the corporate brand. And there is perhaps no better icon of SIA's core values than the Singapore Girl. In the increasingly globalized and high-risk aviation industry, internal communication and training are the first frontiers where the battle for the customer is fought and won—or lost.

◆ KEY TAKEAWAYS ◆

- Employees may be the most important audience for a firm's corporate branding efforts.
- Internal communication (and training) can foster employees' internalization of brand values, which bolsters employees' commitment to enact brand-supporting behaviors.
- By incorporating core values into employees' key touch points, a firm can infuse these values into employees to the extent that they "live" these values.
- It is important to develop communication channels that are tailored to the needs of specific internal stakeholders.
- It is imperative to put in place an evaluation system that ensures behavior is aligned with core values.
- Firms should reinforce the alignment of personal with corporate values throughout the employee's term of employment.

Notes

1. This chapter is an edited version of the original article: Chong, M. (2007). The role of internal communication in infusing corporate values and delivering brand promise: Singapore Airlines' experience. *Corporate Reputation Review*, **10**(3), 201–12.
2. A value is "an enduring belief that a specific mode of conduct or end-state of existence is personally or socially preferable to an opposite or converse mode of conduct or end-state of existence" (Rokeach, 1973, p5).

References

Ackerman, L.D. (2000). *Identity is Destiny: Leadership and the Roots of Value Creation*. San Francisco: Berrett-Koehler Publishers.

Andriopoulos, C. and Gotsi, M. (2001). "Living" the corporate identity: case studies from the creative industry. *Corporate Reputation Review*, **4**(2), 144–54.

Argenti, P.A. and Forman, J. (2002). *The Power of Corporate Communication*. New York: McGraw–Hill.

Ashforth, B.E. and Mael, F. (1989). Social identity theory and the organization. *Academy of Management Review*, **14**(1), 20–39.

Batey, I. (2002). *Asian Branding: A Great Way to Fly*. Singapore: Prentice Hall.

Bennis, W. (1997). Becoming a leader of leaders. In: R. Gibson (ed.), *Rethinking the Future*. London: Nicholas Brealy Publishing, p148–63.

Bettencourt, L.A. and Brown, S. (1997). Contact employees: relationships among workplace fairness, job satisfaction, and pro-social service behaviors. *Journal of Retailing*, **73**(1), 39–61.

Camp, L. (1996). Latest thinking on optimization of brand use in financial services marketing. *Journal of Brand Management*, 3(4), 241–7.

Cheney, G. (1983). On the various and changing meanings of organizational membership: a field study of organizational identification. *Communication Monographs*, **50**, 342–62.

Christensen, L.T. and Askegaard, S. (2001). Corporate identity and corporate image revisited. *European Journal of Marketing*, **35**(3/4), 292–315.

Cleaver, C. (1999). Brands as the catalyst. *Journal of Brand Management*, **6**(5), 309–12.

Collins, J. and Porras, J.I. (2002). *Built to Last: Successful Habits of Visionary Companies*. New York: HarperCollins Publishers.

Davies, G. and Chun, R. (2002). Gaps between the internal and external perceptions of the corporate brand. *Corporate Reputation Review*, **5**(2/3), 144–58.

Davis, B. (1996). Why Singapore Airlines is the world's most profitable airline. *Asian Business Review*, December, 34–7.

de Chernatony, L. (1999). Brand management through narrowing the gap between brand identity and brand reputation. *Journal of Marketing Management*, **15**(1–3), 157–79.

de Chernatony, L. (2002). Would a brand smell any sweeter by a corporate name? *Corporate Reputation Review*, **5**(2/3), 114–32.

de Chernatony, L. and Dall'Olmo Riley, F. (1999). Experts' views about defining service brands and the principles of services branding. *Journal of Business Research*, **46**(2), 181–92.

de Chernatony, L. and Drury, S. (2004). Identifying and sustaining services brands' values. *Journal of Marketing Communications*, **10**(2), 73–93.

Demos, T. (2006). The world's most admired companies. *Fortune*, **153**(4), 33–42.

Dortok, A. (2006). A managerial look at the interaction between internal communication and corporate reputation. *Corporate Reputation Review*, **8**(4), 322–38.

Durgee, J., O'Connar, G. and Veryzer, R. (1996). Observations: translating values into product wants. *Journal of Advertising Research*, **36**(6), 90–9.

Gummeson, E. (1999). *Total Relationship Marketing. Rethinking Marketing Management: From 4Ps to 30Rs.* Oxford: Butterworth Heinemann.

Hardaker, S. and Fill, C. (2005). Corporate services brands: the intellectual and emotional engagement of employees. *Corporate Reputation Review*, **7**(4), 365–76.

Harris, F. and de Chernatony, L. (2001). Corporate branding and corporate brand performance. *European Journal of Marketing*, **35**(3/4), 441–56.

Heracleous, L., Wirtz, J. and Pangarkar, N. (2006). *Flying High in A Competitive Industry: Cost-effective Service Excellence at Singapore Airlines.* Singapore: McGraw-Hill.

Heskett, J. (1987). Lessons in the service sector. *Harvard Business Review*, **65**(2), 118–26.

Jones, J. (1999). The future of banking: implications of branding and loyalty. *Journal of Financial Services Marketing*, **3**(1), 53–66.

Kennedy, S.H. (1977). Nurturing corporate images: total communication or ego trip? *European Journal of Marketing*, **11**(3), 120–64.

Kotter, J. and Heskett, J. (1992). *Corporate Culture and Performance.* New York: The Free Press.

LePla, J.F. and Parker, L.M. (1999). *Integrated Branding: Becoming Brand-driven Through Company-wide Action.* London: Quorum Books.

Liang, D. Money alone can't buy happiness; lack of feedback is why some employees are unhappy. *Today* [Singapore], 2 March 2006.

Martin, G. and Hetrick, S. *Driving Corporate Reputations and Brands From the Inside: A Strategic Role for HR.* Paper presented at the Reputation Institute's 10th International Conference on Corporate Reputation, Image, Identity, and Competitiveness, New York, 25–8 May 2006.

Maxham III, J.B. and Netemeyer, R.G. (2003). Firms reap what they sow: the effects of shared values and perceived organizational justice on customers' evaluations of complaint handling. *Journal of Marketing*, **67**(1), 46–62.

Mitchell, C. (2002). Selling the brand inside. *Harvard Business Review*, **80**(1), 99–105.

Mohammed, S. and Ringseis, E. (2001). Cognitive diversity and consensus in group decision making: the role of inputs, processes, and outcomes. *Organizational Behavior and Human Decision Processes*, **85**(2), 310–35.

Pine II, B.J. and Gilmore, J.H. (1998). Welcome to the experience economy. *Harvard Business Review*, **76**(4), 97–105.

Post, J.E. and Griffin, J.J. (1997). Corporate reputation and external affairs management. *Corporate Reputation Review*, **1**(1/2), 165–71.

Rokeach, M. (1973). *The Nature of Human Values*. New York: The Free Press.

Saxton, K. (1998). Where do reputations come from? *Corporate Reputation Review*, **1**(4), 393–9.

Schein, E.H. (1992). *Organizational Culture and Leadership*. San Francisco: Jossey-Bass.

Schuler, M. (2004). Management of the organizational image: a method for organizational image configuration. *Corporate Reputation Review*, **7**(1), 37–53.

Schultz, M., Hatch, M.J. and Larsen, M.H. (2000). *The Expressive Organization*. New York: Oxford University Press.

Soenen, G. and Moingeon, B. (2002). The five facets of collective identities. Integrating corporate and organizational identity. In: B. Moingeon and G. Soenen (eds.), *Corporate and Organizational Identities: Integrating Strategy, Marketing, Communication, and Organizational Perspectives*. London: Routledge.

Stuart, H. (1999). Towards a definitive model of the corporate identity management process. *Corporate Communications: An International Journal*, **4**(4), 200–7.

Thomson, K., de Chernatony, L., Arganbright, L. and Khan, S. (1999). The buy-in benchmark: how staff understanding and commitment impact brand and business performance. *Journal of Marketing Management*, **8**(15), 819–35.

Thomson, K. and Hecker, L.A. (2000). The business value of buy-in. In: R.J. Varey and B.R. Lewis (eds.), *Internal Marketing: Directions for Management*. London: Routledge.

Vallaster, C. and de Chernatony, L. (2005). Internationalisation of services brands: the role of leadership during the internal brand building process. *Journal of Marketing Management*, **21**(1/2), 181–203.

Wilson, A.M. (2001). Understanding organizational culture and the implications for corporate marketing. *European Journal of Marketing*, **35**(3/4), 353–64.

Zyman, S. (2002). *The End of Advertising As We Know It*. New Jersey: John Wiley.

CHAPTER 8

Five Roles of Social Media in Managing a Company's Reputation Challenges

JEFF RICHARDSON

Executive Summary

The British economist John Kay once observed: "The price of a company's stock depends not on the value of a company but on the market's perception of that value, which is often easier to change than value itself."

Social media now gives voice to every one of your clients—past and present, satisfied and dissatisfied. It gives voice to your prospects as they ask questions, your employees as they share views and information (sometimes sensitive), and your competitors as they present their view of the world. With such breadth of commentary and such a diverse quality of information, it is no wonder social media has the potential to shape the perception of your company's value in a way no other media or conduit has in the past. Not all business people have learnt to respect the power of social media. Those who are disinterested in, ignorant of, and/or apathetic toward the opportunities and risks social media presents behave so at their peril.

This chapter addresses five key roles social media has in managing your company's reputation.

BACKGROUND

In each of the following six case studies, the background is similar. Social media content was impacting the perception of the organization and/or the industry, and the organization needed to understand the facts to then develop an appropriate strategy.

ROLE ONE: DETERMINING THE REALITY

It is often said that what you can measure, you can manage.

When it comes to social media, many people feel that measuring impact is impossible. In fact, not only is it possible, it is often a leading indicator of sentiment, more accurate than old-style research techniques and quicker than mainstream media.

Consider this simple fact: every single sentence shared, statement made, question posed, answer given, or idea planted in social media has passed through computers—many of them. So we know the data is there. It then becomes a matter of extracting and analyzing the information. (Of course, when the writer's profile is locked—or private—the data is not "appropriately" accessible. But then, when in a secure private environment, it is also likely to have minimal impact on the broader community's awareness and perception.)

Does this ability to research and measure impact bring real business value?

Case Study One

Worksafe Victoria is a semi-government body providing information and enforcing local laws relating to workplace safety in the state of Victoria in Australia. With a wealth of information, a clear mandate to inform and support, and a strong presence in above-the-line media, it turned its attention to social media as a growing voice for its audience. In considering its options, some logical questions were raised:

1. Is there an audience in social media for our information?
2. If there is an audience, is there also an opportunity? Do they want what we have?
3. If there is an opportunity, how do we best approach it?

While many organizations jump in, set up an account on their preferred site, and start chatting, Worksafe Victoria chose to research first and to apply the logic of "One strategy, not one hundred tactics." They engaged Online1984, a social media monitoring and analysis tool that applies a statistical measure to relevant mentions.

Determining the reality in social media is not always easy as there are many considerations. Fundamental to any social media analysis is the transference from data to knowledge. Online1984

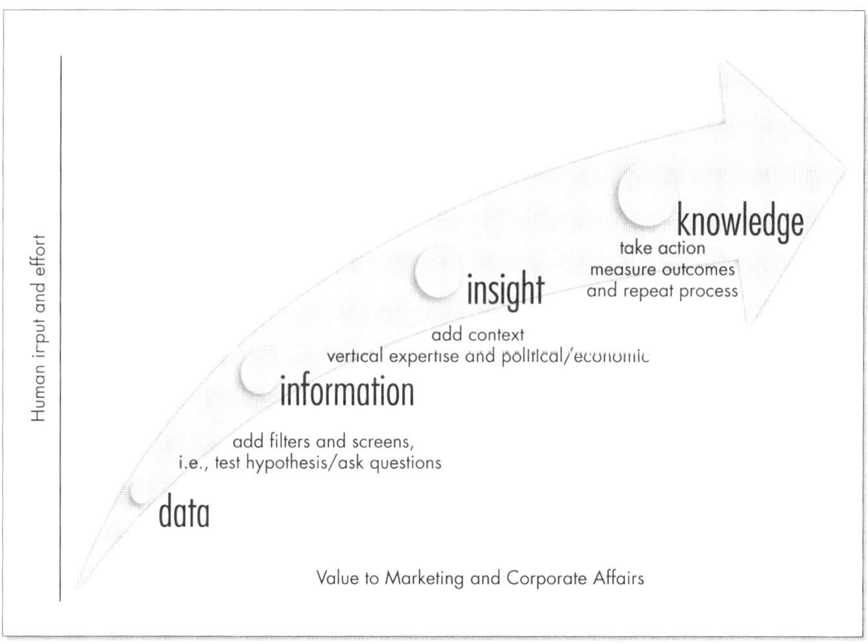

Source: Courtesy of Alan Long, The Online Circle Pty Ltd

took the raw data and converted it to information, insights, and knowledge that Worksafe Victoria then used to develop a logical and structured approach to its entry into the social media space.

The interesting findings included:

1. People were online asking questions and looking for information about "work safety." Since this was a serious and important topic, these people wanted information from a respected information provider.
2. Without a well-structured engagement process by any of the industry leaders, the space was being filled by:
   - Lawyers looking for business ("Have you had an accident? Let us tell you about your options."); and
   - Lesser-known consultants with partial knowledge of work safety issues.
3. The numerical sentiment score applied by Online1984 across all relevant mentions identified a significant lack of enthusiasm for the information currently available. The people seeking help were generally indifferent to the information they found. There was a gap in the conversation.
4. Worksafe Victoria had the opportunity to create a sound thought leadership position by sharing its vast knowledge base via appropriate social media platforms.

How Is the Information Being Used?

At the time of writing, Worksafe Victoria is working to complete a strategic approach to their social media entry. The research highlighted the types of questions being asked and the information sought, the social media environments most relevant for their audience in this context, and the information and information providers currently involved.

This data—combined with Worksafe Victoria's offline research—has given the organization a sound footing for its planning.

Lessons Learned

1. Comprehensive monitoring and thorough analysis of social media is an excellent research tool that can assist in strategic decision making.
2. Applying a numerical value to mentions in social media allows you to differentiate between the influential individuals and the noise.
3. Thought leadership is a powerful position and can be claimed by a lesser body if you allow it.
4. If you do not engage in the social media conversation, it will take place without you.
5. If you do not engage in the social media conversation, you will leave a void and you may not like the people or the information that fills the void.

ROLE TWO: MANAGING THE IMPACT OF PUBLIC COMMENTARY

Bad things can happen online to a company or product's reputation—that is the reality. It is how you deal with it that counts.

Case Study Two

Due to various market pressures, Cottee's Cordial, part of the Schweppes Australia portfolio, embarked upon bold product and packaging changes.

Moving from a two-liter to a one-liter bottle—but retaining the value for the consumer—was always going to result in a degree of confusion and angst from members of the public. Complaints and conversations regarding the mixing difficulty, the value, the inclusion of sucralose, and changes to taste flooded a range of social media sites.

Monitoring identified not only the obvious places such as Facebook and Twitter, but also less likely places such as football club forums and technical forums. Potentially the greatest challenge was that the majority of the conversation, including complaints, was taking place on a Facebook page started and managed by a fan of the product that looked as though it was the official Cottee's Cordial fan page. Fans were asking questions the admin person could not answer. She was ignoring them. They were getting more angry and frustrated.

It was important to Schweppes that it chose to actively engage in the social media conversation rather than ignore it. This, of course, was not as easy as it sounds. The situation presented two separate but linked management challenges:

1. Cottee's Cordial needed to claim ownership of the Facebook page to enable it to effectively manage consumer perception. The company needed to answer consumers' questions and move the community's conversation to a more positive position.
2. In the forums and other environments that the company could not directly control and that had limited space for information, Cottee's Cordial needed to acknowledge the issues raised, invite consumers to visit the micro site that provided more detailed information, and generally demonstrate that it was listening.

In claiming the Facebook page, Cottee's Cordial did not want to be represented as a corporate giant that did not care about the originator of the page. On the contrary, the approach was very much to thank her for her efforts, to acknowledge the job she had done in growing the page, and to offer assistance in dealing with the difficult questions currently pervading the community. Through this approach, the company was able to secure an existing Facebook page, manage the short-term discontent, run promotions, and grow the community further, thus increasing the asset value.

In this context, a key ongoing measure of success for the page is the level of engagement fans have with it. This is normally expressed both as a raw number and as a percentage of the total community. It is one thing having a bunch of people click the "Like" button, leave the page, and never come back or engage with the brand. It is another to have them comment or answer poll questions.

What Happened?

At the time of writing, some challenges still exist, but the online aggression has dropped markedly as consumers have had their issues acknowledged and addressed. The Facebook community has been a great success. It has doubled in size, is more active, and now provides a platform for future promotions and other campaigns.

Lessons Learned

1. Companies no longer own the only voice.
2. Bad things happen—and this will increase, not decrease, over time.
3. Be prepared to get involved—but do it cautiously and strategically.
4. Learn as you go.
5. A healthy online community is determined by its level of engagement in the conversation, not the raw number of fans.
6. A truly healthy community will help protect a brand by speaking on the brand's behalf when it is being attacked online.

ROLE THREE: MANAGING SERVICE PROVIDERS AND/OR STAFF WHO KNOW JUST ENOUGH TO BE DANGEROUS

To many people, managing social media seems easy. Maybe it is the use of the word "social" that lulls them into a false sense of security. But, with so many voices and platforms, strategies and different motivations, social media is not easy to manage. It is different and in many regards a great deal more difficult to manage effectively than traditional forms of media.

Staff and service providers as well as experts in other forms of business communication convince themselves and others that they can meet the company's needs in this area. Unfortunately, many of these people are taking a simplistic approach and simply do not know what they do not know—they are ignorant regarding social media management, but they do not realize it.

Case Study Three

A significant change in the manufacturing process of a popular confectionery product meant that there would be notable changes in texture and taste. Consumer backlash was expected and was accepted as part of the business decision in making the change. However, it was believed the backlash could be minimized with the right marketing communication execution.

The Marketing Department's mainstream advertising agency was called in and given a brief. Their solution—create a bright, fun TV ad that would encourage fans to join them on the similarly bright, fun Facebook page. The Facebook page would have a game on it and, in theory, lots of fun conversation. But neither the TV ad nor the Facebook page would have any reference to the changes the customer was bound to notice.

The Marketing team and their mainstream agency convinced themselves their customers would be so happy with the fun they could have on the Facebook page that the changes in the product would not be a concern.

What Happened?

The company, through its expensive TV ad and placements, funded the creation of an environment (the Facebook page) where disgruntled consumers who had previously loved the product could share their disappointment and angst at the change in the product. A very angry and very vocal Facebook community continuously posted negative comments about the product changes and related issues.

Because this Facebook page now gave a voice and an audience to the disgruntled consumers, the issue flared much more than it would have otherwise. Corporate Affairs and the specialist social media management agency became involved when it became apparent the brand was being severely damaged and that the mainstream agency, inexperienced in social media management, was not able to moderate this tricky situation.

The company needed to convert this discontented and angry place into the happy, fun Facebook page it was originally intended to be and that it felt the product deserved.

How Did the Company Deal with This Situation?

Often, in difficult social media environments, the temptation is to jump in and start answering back, deleting posts that do not please the admin people, and generally overtly controlling the community. This very tactical approach has little structure and rarely achieves the intended goals.

Rather than a tactical response, the company followed a process of watching, identifying, and segmenting the audience before managing each segment appropriately. As in real life, in social media each person has his own interests, concerns, and motivations. Treating the community as a single homogeneous group is a common error in social media management that limits opportunity and increases risk.

On this occasion, it was essential to identify the aggressors on the page that were truly aggrieved at the product changes, those that were vocal with other concerns such as job losses, the trolls, and potentially the frauds. Having identified the key individuals and their motivations, the company set in place a communication process to address the genuinely aggrieved, quieten the trolls and fraudsters, and give a voice to the silent majority who still loved the product but who had not been prepared to rally against the aggressors—they were paralyzed by the "bystander effect." The following schematic demonstrates this process:

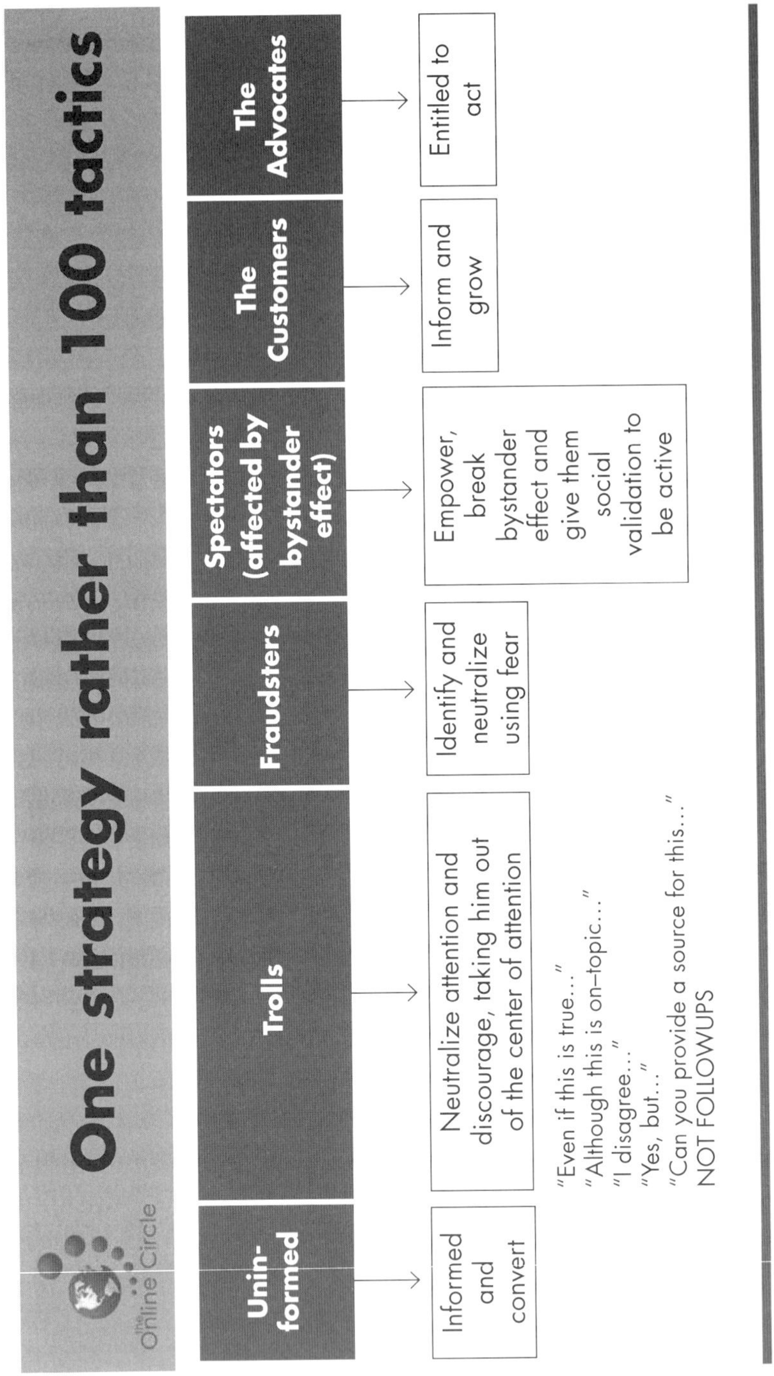

Source: Courtesy of Lucio Ribeiro, The Online Circle Pty Ltd

Lessons Learned

1. Hiding the facts is much harder today than it was. And, when facts are found out by others, they are much more easily spread. Face the reality and engage in the truth.
2. Some service providers, who are experts in other areas, take on social media management as an extension of their services. But they do not understand the subtleties of the space—and worse, they do not know what they do not know.
3. A client who does not question the service provider carefully enough can find themselves in the wrong place and the service provider out of its depth.
4. As with other business communication processes, strategy leads and tactics follow. Do not let tactics lead.
5. A Facebook page is not always the answer.
6. Respect the power of social media and recognize it can work against you just as easily as it can work for you.
7. When it comes to social media, you cannot afford to be flippant or simplistic.

ROLE FOUR: IDENTIFYING INTENTIONAL SUBTERFUGE, MISREPRESENTATION OF FACTS, AND FRAUDULENT COMPETITIVE ACTIVITY DESIGNED TO HARM YOUR BRAND

Sometimes, we bring troubles upon ourselves (with the help of staff and service providers). Other times, trouble is brought upon us aggressively and with malicious intent.

Case Study Four

An international manufacturer of consumables found this out the hard way when a competitor set out to discredit the brand via social media.

During a difficult time when the manufacturer was coming under scrutiny regarding its manufacturing process and ingredients, it noted that a small number of protagonists involved in the social media conversation appeared to have a greater knowledge than would be expected from a normal member of the public and were very proactive in their criticism. Using a forensic Internet investigations process, the company studied the conversations, comments, and behaviors of the suspects and the environments in which they were taking place.

The goal was to identify trends in behavior, disproportionate contributions in terms of information and/or fervor, and the beginnings of troublesome conversations where they had been of no prior interest. Further forensics then profiled the individuals concerned.

In this case, monitoring their behavior in peripheral social media sites, tracking their ISP location, and other tactics provided enough information to reaffirm the suspicion that they may well be competitors acting to intentionally damage the company's reputation. The investigation was able to provide the Legal Department with all the information needed for them to explore the option of taking legal action.

In a similar but separate situation, an aggressive and knowledgeable participant in a social media community turned out to be a journalist for a well-known media outlet. A simple view of her profile did not disclose this, and an inexperienced social media analyst may not have researched beyond the profile to identify the real risk involved in dismissing this person too lightly or arguing with her ineffectually.

Lessons Learned

1. Not all people online are what they seem.
2. If something feels wrong, it very possibly is.
3. The ability for someone to hide his true self and misrepresent himself and the facts is, unfortunately, very

easy online. And more unfortunate is that your fans and customers most often won't be able to tell the difference and will take these people at face value.

4. Internet forensics investigations allow you to learn more than the basics about suspect individuals and potentially build a legal case.
5. People who are speaking against you with detailed knowledge and information may have a separate agenda as competitors or disgruntled employees.
6. Internet forensics can be an important part of your overall ongoing analysis of your online brand representation.

ROLE FIVE: MANAGING STAFF, INCLUDING EDUCATION, TRAINING, AND MONITORING

It is surprisingly common to find that employees do not understand the implications of their actions within the social media space. And when their actions reference their employer in some way, it relates specifically to managing the company's reputation.

Case Study Five: Criticizing the Employer Online

Monitoring across international borders for a global company, the Online1984 social media monitoring and analysis service identified two separate staff-oriented concerns in two separate countries.

Following decisions regarding site closures, some staff took it upon themselves to create video parodies of the company and the decisions made and to post those videos on YouTube. The videos were unflattering and clearly referenced the client company. The information in the video was biased, but for viewers of the video this was all they knew. Using a simple, coordinated Internet forensics process enabled the tracking of the original posters of the video. The information was passed to the client for next steps, which included discussions with the staff and having the video taken down.

In a separate incident, three colleagues were having what they assumed was a private conversation as they criticized their workplace as "the worst place in the world to work." The conversation was on a Facebook page open to the public, and so it was in the public domain. Once Online1984 monitoring discovered it and reported it to the client, management was able to engage with and address the employees' concerns in a way that would not have been possible if the incident had not come to light.

In each of the above instances, there was a direct and potentially serious negative impact on the company's reputation. The situations needed to be addressed by Corporate Affairs with Human Resources' involvement.

Case Study Six: Fragmentation of a Social Media Presence

Not all employee-related challenges, however, are due to malicious intent, anger, or angst.

A local government in Australia engaged The Online Circle to complete an audit of its social media exposure and to recommend a best-practice approach moving forward. The audit uncovered a range of disparate Facebook pages, Twitter accounts, video uploads, and so forth executed by employees actively trying to present their council facility in a positive way.

Without the employees realizing it, their simplistic approach resulted in a fragmentation of assets for the council and an incongruent representation to the public. There was no consistency of tone, message, or information. The opportunity to cross-reference between the pages and other mentions was lost, and potential synergies were not realized.

And, most serious of all, the individual employees acting without guidance or full understanding were exposing themselves and their employer to legal liability. It is commonly accepted that the administrator of a social media environment such as a company's Facebook fan page is legally liable for all content, including that posted by others. The logic is that the administrator of the page has editorial control. This has now been tested and proven in a number of test cases.

The recommended best-practice approach for the client moving forward now includes a centralization of assets. This does not mean the existing assets will be closed down, but that their management will be overseen via a central structure. This central structure will be managed through Corporate Affairs and will ensure consistent management guidelines for objectives, measurement, and reporting in addition to the newly consistent tone and information.

Training Staff

Training of their staff will be a part of the council's best-practice approach. A three-tiered training and certification process will comprise:

1. An introduction to social media for all staff;
2. Intermediary training to allow support staff to responsibly engage online on behalf of the council; and
3. Advanced training for those staff who are to be ultimately responsible for individual council social media assets, such as a Facebook page.

This will ensure:

1. All staff are aware of the implications of their actions; and
2. The team members who do engage online on behalf of the council are up to date with the options, the pitfalls, the expectations, and best-practice management.

Lessons Learned

1. When it comes to social media, your staff do not necessarily understand the impact of their actions.
2. Corporate Affairs should organize company-wide education of staff as to the perils of social media.

3. Further training and certification of staff who actively manage company assets will help ensure consistency in management, including measurements against stated objectives.
4. Social media monitoring and analysis may provide unexpected insights helpful to staff management decision making.
5. Best-practice social media execution involves centralization, not fragmentation, to maximize consistency and synergy.

HOW SHOULD SOCIAL MEDIA BE MANAGED, AND BY WHICH DEPARTMENT(S)?

Because of social media's broad reach, the varied platforms, and the multiple potential uses, it is inevitable that many areas of a large business will have some involvement in social media management:

1. Marketing's role is to promote the brand, generate sales (or leads), and generally push the boundaries. Social media provides many avenues for proactive promotional messaging.
2. Consumer Insights teams are beginning to appreciate the quality and speed of research findings that are coming through high-quality social media monitoring and analysis.
3. Consumer Relations departments are benefiting from social media both in terms of responding to customer concerns and in identifying potential issues before they get out of control.
4. The sales team may have an interest in connecting with clients on a personal level through platforms such as Facebook and LinkedIn. This comes with risks that many will not have considered.

5. The Legal Department will be concerned about risk. A realistic management approach will need to balance that risk with opportunity.
6. Human Resources may recognize social media as an advertising opportunity to attract the best talent as well as a great resource tool to find out more about applicants. Social media can be resource-intensive and skill-dependent, and so this will also involve Human Resources.

But the overriding consideration has to be managing a company's overall reputation and caring for the Master Brand. This is best managed by Corporate Affairs.

Without doubt, the business model for social media management that I have seen work best in large companies is where Corporate Affairs provides the lead role. Other departments can act largely autonomously, but within the larger framework and guidelines established and administered by Corporate Affairs. This ongoing administration encompasses:

1. An overall responsibility for the company's reputation
2. A risk planning process
3. Education for all staff and further training and certification for those who wish to actively represent the organization in social media
4. Maintaining up-to-date knowledge of this fast-changing medium
5. Providing a structure for consistency that other departments follow:
    - Clear objectives for their use of social media and measures against those objectives
    - Exit strategies from promotional activities
    - Campaign-based risk analysis and planning
    - Content subject area analysis

The reference to others acting largely autonomously is important. Speed is often an issue in social media management. The need for individual brands to incorporate their unique positioning and tone is essential. Creativity and flexibility are strengths in this medium.

And, with the right larger framework and guidelines in place, your company can get on with taming this beast, confident you have done all you can to maximize the opportunities and manage the risk.

◆ KEY TAKEAWAYS ◆

The case studies in this chapter demonstrate what a beast social media can be and how a company's reputation is now in the hands of the many. Further, the users of social media—and therefore your audience—are not just your customers, but also:

- Politicians
- Lobby groups
- Online influencers
- Public figures interested in your product or services
- The media
- Community partners
- Business partners
- Suppliers
- Competitors
- Shareholders

9

CHAPTER

Corporate Affairs in India—Moving from a Shareholder to a Stakeholder World

OPHIRA SAMUEL-BHATIA

Executive Summary

This chapter examines the changes, challenges, and opportunities for building reputation and business success in the world's largest democracy—India. With 350 million members in the Indian middle class and the country's growing affluence, India is now one of the most powerful and attractive consumer markets in the world. At the same time, India continues to be challenged on the other end of the socio-economic spectrum with low levels of literacy, poor access to affordable health care, poor infrastructure, and 400 million citizens living below the poverty line. Companies are encouraged to keep these paradoxes and sensitivities in mind when operating in this market, as well as the key imperatives they should adopt when building reputation and communication programs in India.

India's socio-political environment is defined by a rise in judicial activism and calls for greater scrutiny of ethical practices across all institutions, an explosion of digital media and citizen journalism, and rising demands of corporate competitiveness in one of the most attractive growth markets in the world. These elements create a "perfect storm" of opportunities for India's Corporate Affairs professionals to play a defining role in building strong reputations for corporations and strengthening society's trust in these companies.

BACKGROUND

Corporate Affairs in India is—by and large—still either synonymous with media relations or identified with "fixing," a sign of the relative immaturity of the sector. The recent revelations[1] of a Corporate Affairs professional attempting to influence government decision making at the behest of certain business interests has reinforced this image.

The industry is, in the main, limited to providing such relatively unsophisticated services as much by clients restricting Corporate Affairs thinking to these services as by Corporate Affairs professionals focusing largely on patchwork execution rather than on strategic achievement. This effectively curtails the service offering, with price as the major variable (at the expense of strategic efficacy or value). Media clips are the primary deliverable, with little attention paid to content. As a cost center delivering little strategic value, Corporate Affairs then becomes a game of the lowest bidder—Corporate Affairs agencies take on vendor status, while Corporate Affairs departments focus on cost management via the frequent staging of competitive reviews.

Indeed, Indian Corporate Affairs has long been the poor cousin of Advertising and Marketing, rather than a strategic partner and influencer of both. However, there has been a slow change in attitude in recent years, largely driven by new forces at work in Indian society—market competitiveness, information technology, and increasing demands from civil society and government regulators for transparency, accountability, and responsible corporate citizenship.

CREEPING CHANGE

Companies in India are operating in a quicksand of change driven by the information age, globalization, and the emergence of a vast new body of stakeholders from civil society. The top-down model of communication no longer works in this new era of mindful citizenship and unbridled information exchange on digital platforms. The demand for transparency is being pushed by global and national audiences that require new levels of creativity and engagement in reputation building.

The focus of Corporate Affairs has shifted from managing perceptions to driving conversations, from merely building media relations to building a robust network of well-informed influencers and participants. As digital information platforms become more popular—even in rural India, through the electronic networks provided by government and nongovernmental organizations (NGOs)—conversations and demands for accountability are on the rise. Thus, the focus has shifted from managing media in a few metro centers to managing reputations with diverse audiences in a spectrum of markets—global, urban, rural, and semi-rural. White goods manufacturers, telecom service providers, and insurers are today targeting the rural Indian market more than the urban centers; on the other hand, environment-friendly energy technology companies and green car manufacturers are looking to build credibility in global rather than domestic markets.

THE DIGITAL INFLUENCE

Digital communication is broadly recognized as the "next big thing," taking away some of the overwhelming focus on communicating through mainstream media such as print publications, television, and radio.

The number of Internet users in India is growing at over ten per cent annually (Gavane, 2011); about 75 per cent of existing users are in the 15- to 34-year-old age group, spending an average of 16 hours a week online—two hours more than the time spent viewing TV (*The Times of India*, 2011). Search is the most popular online activity, followed closely by social networking (Gavane, 2011). Reportedly, there are about 30 million Indian users of Facebook (Gavane, 2011), 21 million registered users of YouTube, and four million on Twitter (Google DoubleClick Ad Planner, 2011).

Mobile phone use—with more than 851 million subscriptions as of June 2011—has revolutionized communication (Wikipedia, 2011). It has had a direct impact on consumerism, information sharing, accessibility, and regional growth and is playing a key role in marketing and communication. It has opened up rural markets to corporate organizations looking for markets beyond the metros.

For Corporate Affairs professionals, these developments require changes in media strategies, notwithstanding India's 330 million newspaper readers (Kohli-Khandekar, 2011), television available in 522 million homes (Media Research Users Council and Hansa Research, 2011), and even larger radio audiences. Digital media, however, encourages two-way communication and thus demands more from corporate communicators in terms of responsiveness and transparency. This represents both a challenge and an opportunity for Corporate Affairs.

THE CIVIL SOCIETY FACTOR

Corporate organizations are increasingly being compelled to answer to the large number of NGOs and other civil society organizations, and be responsive to the growing demands for accountability from both national and state regulatory bodies and international agencies. There has been greater emphasis on the effective implementation of laws, such as the Consumer Protection Act, 1996, and the Right to Information Act of 2005. Judicial activism has also brought businesses under scrutiny for ethical business practices and adherence to principles of social responsibility. This, in turn, has led to the spotlight of public inquiry being turned on the degree of sustainability of manufacturing and other business processes.

Media interest in business has widened from news of alliances, mergers, acquisitions, expansions, and boardroom conflicts to consumer affairs as well as environmental and ethical practices. For businesses, it has become imperative to develop and sustain a good reputation so as to successfully enter capital markets (both in India and abroad), successfully meet competition, and win customer loyalty. These developments have led to a spurt in the demand for Corporate Affairs.

THE DEMANDS OF MARKET COMPETITIVENESS

Along with these developments, the need to demonstrate international competitiveness is likely to create a "perfect storm" in the business environment, bringing in its wake a dramatic change in Indian Corporate Affairs. The magical myth of a 350-million-strong middle class in India has now been recast. The National Council for Applied Economic Research reported in February 2011 that India had 31.4 million middle class households—or around 160 million middle class individuals—and projected that the number would rise to 53.3 million households by 2015-6, translating into 267 million individuals (*The Economic Times [India]*, 2011).

While this segment is the prime market for all kinds of products and services, India continues to be challenged by enduring developmental issues—entrenched poverty, low levels of literacy, poor access to health care, inadequate infrastructure, and social inequities, with over 410 million below the poverty line living on less than US$1.35 a day (World Bank, 2011). Companies and businesses—whether they are in the consumer products space, manufacturing, or infrastructure—must consider this demographic inequity to develop programs or messages that will be in sync with the sensitivities of the Indian market.

Equally, businesses cannot ignore regional disparities, in particular the aspirations of the small towns and cities. Instead of the gradual "trickle down" from metros to small towns that was the norm, now it is the aspirations of small towns that are driving trends across India and providing the fuel for the Indian economic surge.

It is no wonder that today India is of significant interest to the widest range of businesses. Already a massive economy (the fourth-largest in terms of purchasing power parity), Goldman Sachs has projected that India will grow fourfold by 2020 and that it will be larger than the US economy by 2043 (Poddar and Yi, 2007).

Given India's growth priorities and development environment, businesses need more than ever to communicate—to launch products and services; position the company's financial performance through investor relations; highlight business growth and strategy, market entries, mergers, and acquisitions; build awareness about a program or platform; and during a crisis or emergency.

THE CORPORATE AFFAIRS FACTOR

All these developments have led to the demand for a new generation of Corporate Affairs professionals capable of looking at the entire spectrum of stakeholders—media, analysts, opinion leaders, regulators, and civil society—who together demand responsiveness, transparency, and information. Corporate Affairs professionals, therefore, are becoming partners in helping their organizations and clients realize their business goals.

Given the complexity of the environment and the changing forces, communicating right and building a defined reputation has become a core of successful business strategies. But Corporate Affairs can be *right* only with the right content and "feel" for the business, when it becomes a C-suite and boardroom-level tool.

India's Corporate Affairs professionals have the opportunity to play a defining role in building the corporate reputation of businesses. However, it has become increasingly challenging to identify target audiences and messages in an environment that has become steadily more complex. In today's multi-stakeholder world, communicators are compelled to take cognizance not only of direct audiences, but also a plethora of influencers to those audiences and the multiple channels to reach these multiple audiences and influencers!

Some key imperatives of a smart communication program are discussed below.

Recognizing Stakeholders Beyond the Shareholder

The "Corporate Affairs Officers" (they were earlier called "Public Relations Officers") of yesteryear had one mandate: to share information about the company, because these companies were often publicly listed. Today, besides shareholders, companies recognize that the target audience has grown. Consumers, partners, experts, regulators, NGOs and other civil society players, media persons, and employees are all looking for information.

Any effective communication program now needs to consider all these stakeholders and the impact that the business has on them. It is no longer enough to communicate key messages—it is critical to engage in a conversation. Stakeholders expect a relationship with companies and brands. Therefore, there is a need to build advocates for a brand or business over a longer period of time.

Doing Good and Doing Right

This is an era of citizenship, and companies are now evaluating performance through the lens of the triple bottom line. Businesses are now accountable for more than making money—they need to evaluate their impact on the society in which they operate and contribute to reducing that impact or addressing it. The Indian arm of PepsiCo became the first of the company's global units environment than it consumed and become water positive. The ICICI Group has taken financial inclusion as a key area of focus. The discussion is also shifting away from pure "giving" to working with the community and engaging it. So, the famed Project Shakti of Hindustan Unilever

Limited helps women in rural India to set up small businesses as direct-to-consumer retailers. The scheme equips women with business skills, offers them a way out of poverty, and creates a crucial new distribution channel for Unilever products in the large and fast-growing global market of low-spending consumers.

Working with the Government

The Corporate Affairs practitioner used to consider government relations as "fixing" and "file pushing." While this practice still exists, a more professional, strategic approach has developed where Corporate Affairs works to map issues and key stakeholders, engage at a strategic level on the basis of these issues, and inform the debate. The function has moved beyond fixing meetings or pushing through agendas—it has instead become more strategic to include a longer-term view on providing perspectives, experiences, and expertise to guide the development of rules and laws.

INDIAN CORPORATE AFFAIRS TODAY: THE IMPERATIVES

What can be done to build a robust corporate brand, especially given the ever-changing environment in India and the impact of global changes?

Define the Company

A company or brand must have clear responses on questions such as the business it is in, its product or service offering, its lines of business, its industry environment, its value system, and its beliefs. This needs to be translated into a narrative that is embedded within the organization so that everyone—both within and outside the organization—speaks the same language.

Identify Stakeholders

It is essential to map out stakeholders and their level of influence in the company's stakeholder universe. The company can then work on specific channels to reach out to these stakeholders.

Engage in the New Media Landscape

Digital social media provides a direct two-way communication platform with stakeholders. It also offers the highest community, consumer, and mobile engagement among all media. This is the new Media Cloverleaf, according to Richard Edelman, CEO of the world's largest independent public relations firm.

Engage Employees

Employees are today the most crucial voices for a business or company. Very often, employees have access to diverse audiences and geographies. It is therefore imperative for the communication team to partner closely with Human Resources.

Prepare for Crises

Crisis response preparedness is crucial for companies. The digital platform has redefined communication—journalists alone no longer control the flow of conversation; citizen journalists have taken over. For example, in November 2010, the 2G telecom scam broke online in India two days before it made the mainline papers. What it means is that companies cannot wait until a crisis to create an engaged and credible influencer community. Instead, companies and their Corporate Affairs teams must work in "times of peace" to identify influencers in both the physical and digital worlds and cultivate them through active engagement. These influencers can become advocates and tell the company story in times of crisis as credible third-party sources.

Engage with the Fifth Estate: NGOs

About 3.3 million active NGOs were reported to be operating in India at the end of 2009. This essentially means India has one NGO for every 400 people (Shukla, 2010). Today, NGO activism is a crucial element of business planning. Identifying key NGO influencers and engaging in an active dialogue with them on a regular basis is critical for certain industries such as food (as evidenced in the Coke and Pepsi adulteration issue with the Centre for Science and Environment in 2006), energy, infrastructure, and mining, among others. NGO partnerships—if well developed—can also help companies develop programs to reach out to communities.

However, according to the Edelman Trust Barometer 2011, Indians are more trusting of business than of NGOs (of all the people surveyed from India, 70 per cent trust business whereas 61 trust NGOs), in contrast to most other APAC countries where trust is equal or NGOs are more trusted.

Maintain Messaging Consistency

Businesses and companies must define themselves and develop consistent messaging to communicate their vision, values, commitment to the country, and long-term plans. This consistent messaging must reflect the CEO's agenda.

Speak Up

The Edelman Trust Barometer 2011 found that 78 per cent (up by 20 per cent from 2010) of those surveyed in India look to the CEO of a company as the most trusted source of information, followed by the technical experts from the company, and then by external experts. This means that communication needs to be a critical agenda for CEOs. It also means that a company's senior leadership needs to be the face of the company.

Develop Platforms

A person needs to see or hear something five times in different places from a range of spokespeople before believing it. Therefore, crucial to the process is the identification of relevant platforms and developing these for the long term. Ernst and Young, for example, has built awards, events, and thought leadership around the entrepreneurship platform, thus meeting its business needs and communicating its role as a driver of business growth and entrepreneurship.

Mobilize Influencers

Companies would do well to engage stakeholders by bringing them together in social networks and providing them with the opportunity to give content and feedback. It is critical to leverage these influencers (people who are already talking about the company) to amplify messages within the mainstream and online media. It is no longer enough to only communicate to influencers—companies must also encourage them to create conversations, communicate with one another, and inform these conversations.

TODAY

The process of building reputations and trust in a corporation is—worldwide—a long-term, planned, and inclusive process. In India, the CEO and other business leaders play a more critical role in this process than is common in the West. Trust in corporate leaders is high, and these leaders are regarded as the most reliable spokespeople for the business.

Media relations for Corporate Affairs also hinges largely on the voices of corporate spokespeople. Therefore, development of skills in media relations is crucial for corporate leaders.

Businesses today have to contend increasingly with the external world—government, regulators, experts, NGOs, and consumers.

Not only do all these stakeholders influence the credibility of the corporate entity, they impact its operations. Regulators are becoming increasingly more proactive and are obvious influencers in the fortunes of business. Less obvious are the roles of experts and NGOs, who have become increasingly more active as "conscience keepers," questioning corporate entities on issues of social and environmental impact, technical sustainability and claims, and safety. Consumers have always played a key role in building trust and reputation; today, they are also more demanding with regard to safety and other standards, as awareness of health, safety, and the environment has increased.

Thus, managing the Corporate Affairs portfolio requires developing new skill sets, understanding various issues and stakeholder behaviors, and addressing these with information disseminated through predetermined channels. These changes are being driven and determined by an unprecedented call for governance, transparency, and access to information.

Corporate Affairs is at the cusp of maturity in India. The role of a communications consultancy has moved from being tactical to strategic. In a multi-stakeholder world—and with the emergence of digital media where consumers, partners, and others increasingly rely on the online space to make purchasing and business decisions—communication must address this complex need and environment.

This is the time in India for professional Public Relations services—businesses and corporations need smart Corporate Affairs programs that will help them stand out, stand up, and be noticed. A one-way mode of interaction is not viable or acceptable, especially in a complex, interconnected, and fragmented environment made up of varied cultures, people, and languages.

Corporate Affairs is fast redefining itself to meet the challenges facing the modern corporation in India. Professionalism, research, transparency, and informed influence are becoming key words, as corporations engage with an expansive world of stakeholders to build and sustain trust and reputation and long-term value add.

Note

1. These refer to the 2G spectrum scam in 2008—where rules and procedures were flouted when 2G licenses were issued to private telecommunication companies at throwaway prices—and costing the Indian government approximately US$39 billion (Rs 176,000 crores). Former Telecom Minister, A. Raja, was charged along with several other high-profile political and business leaders and journalists. The scam came to light in November 2010, when taped conversations (recorded by the Indian Income Tax Department in 2008–9) between a high-profile public relations professional and corporate lobbyist revealed malpractices in the allocation of the 2G licenses.

References

Gavane, K. *State of the Internet in India.* comScore, Inc., 7 June 2011. Retrieved from http://www.comscore.com/Press_Events/Presentations_Whitepapers/2011/State_of_the_Internet_in_India.

Google DoubleClick Ad Planner, August 2011.

Google turns a page in India with SMB Ad push. *The Times of India*, 19 April 2011.

India's middle class population to touch 267 million in 5 years. *The Economic Times* [India], 6 February 2011.

Kohli-Khandekar, V. Can Indian newspapers survive the Net? *Business Standard* [India], 21 June 2011.

Media Research Users Council and Hansa Research. (2011). *Indian Cable and Satellite TV Reach Rises By 17.9 per cent.* Retrieved from http://dream-dth.com/Forum/Thread-Update-Indian-cable-and-satellite-TV-reach-rises-by-17-9.

Poddar, T. and Yi, E. (2007). *India's Rising Growth Potential.* Goldman Sachs Global Economics Paper 152. Retrieved from http://www.usindiafriendship.net/viewpoints1/Indias_Rising_Growth_Potential.pdf.

Shukla, A. The twist in India's NGO tale: strong numbers, low transparency. *The Indian Express*, 17 August 2010.

Wikipedia. *Communications in India.* Retrieved from http://en.wikipedia.org/wiki/Communications_in_India.

World Bank. *India Country Overview—September 2011.* Retrieved from http://www.worldbank.org.in/WBSITE/EXTERNAL/COUNTRIES/SOUTHASIAEXT/INDIAEXTN/0,,contentMDK:20195738~pagePK:141137~ piPK:141127~theSitePK:295584,00.html.

10

CHAPTER

Corporate Affairs in China

BASSKARAN NAIR

Executive Summary

This chapter looks at several communication issues unique to China. Among these issues are the role of soft power in China's brand equity, the negative domestic events that mar the country's reputation, and the increasing impact and influence of social media in China's communication structure. It lists some corporate communication initiatives that international firms can adopt when operating in China. It concludes that there are great corporate communication opportunities there for both multinational firms and China's own companies.

BACKGROUND

This essay looks at several salient communication issues: some basic precepts unique to China; the role of mega events (such as the 2008 Beijing Olympics) in communicating to the world that China has arrived; the role of soft power in projecting China's brand equity; the negative domestic events that mar China's reputation; and the important role of social media in the communication structure in China. At all times, the senior executive must pay particular attention to domestic issues and party politics. The sharp rural-urban divide and ensuing social inequalities have created widespread anger—the calls in 2011 for a "Jasmine Revolution" in China are a product of this resentment. The party keeps a tight lid on domestic issues, and no international demands (to revalue the yuan currency, for example) are considered seriously by the Chinese Communist Party if they trigger off domestic upheaval. So, it is advisable that the C-suite understands and considers these issues, perhaps within the context of public affairs advisory and strategies.

LEVERAGE OFF MAJOR EVENTS

Multinational companies will find that it is relatively easy to communicate to urban and affluent China about international brands and global products. However, to have effective reach, one must consider events that fit the needs of the government or the local authorities in the various provinces, cities, or towns. When Shanghai held the 2010 World Expo, many multinationals tailored their programs to meet the needs of the Shanghai authorities.

For example, Singapore-headquartered real-estate developer CapitaLand Group organized a "Hand in Hand 20.10" program to inspire underprivileged children in China to strive toward a better life, in line with the Shanghai World Expo's theme of "Better City, Better Life." The company chose to reach out to 2,010 underprivileged children drawn from several provinces in China, as the year 2010 marked not only 20 years of diplomatic relations between Singapore and China, but also CapitaLand's tenth anniversary in China. The "Hand in Hand 20.10" community education program ran from May to August 2010. During that period, close to 1,000 CapitaLand and public volunteers accompanied underprivileged children to visit the Shanghai World Expo. Working closely with Shanghai Business Media Group as partner, CapitaLand generated immense publicity across China and fulfilled the goals of the local government (the Shanghai Municipality in this case).

CapitaLand organized the "Hand in Hand 20.10" program for underprivileged children to be in line with the Shanghai Expo's theme of "Better City, Better Life."
Source: Courtesy of CapitaLand Limited

Similarly, US multinationals such as General Electric (GE) got involved in the 2008 Beijing Olympics. GE's US$700-million sponsorship of the Games strengthened the company's long term relationship with China, where it does more than US$4 billion worth of business.

Coca-Cola Co., Samsung Group, and Lenovo paid millions of dollars for the exclusive rights to sponsor the 2008 Beijing Olympics torch relay. Coca-Cola threw a giant party when the torch landed in Hainan. It also unveiled a TV commercial featuring a giant red carpet being rolled out for the torch from the top of Mount Everest. These efforts have paid off for Coca-Cola, as

China is now one of the largest markets for several of its brands. Likewise, Lenovo's US$100-million-plus sponsorship of the Games provided a massive brand boost for the company.

BE MINDFUL OF INALIENABLE TRUTHS

It is important to be mindful of potential downsides. Even modern-minded Chinese people—especially politicians—revert to Maoist language when questions of territorial integrity are touched upon. For instance, the Chinese are single-minded about the Dalai Lama being a negative factor. An interesting public affairs case is Carrefour's operations in China. Carrefour is a foreign firm that has been in China since 1995, and its brand name is almost synonymous with supermarkets in China. From coastal Qingdao to inland Urumqi, "Jia Le Fu"—the Chinese name of Carrefour—means "happy and lucky family;" it is a byword for "downtown" in many second- and third-tier Chinese cities. Despite such a strong brand position, the Chinese called for a boycott of Carrefour in 2008 after rumors spread that the company had backed the Dalai Lama during the pro-Tibet protests at the Olympic torch relay in Paris.

Similarly, the Chinese feel that Taiwan is an inalienable part of China and that they should be willing to shed blood to keep the country together. Supporters of Taiwanese independence are called "splittists." China even threatens trade sanctions whenever the United States sells weapons to Taiwan. The Chinese government has been prepared to cancel meetings and blacklist offending countries and their firms from doing business in China.

Given China's history of being the "Middle Kingdom" generations ago, the Chinese government and the Chinese people's reaction to slights (or perceived slights) exceeds the alleged offence. For instance, China pulled out of an annual summit with the European Union when the French president, Nicolas Sarkozy, met the Dalai Lama. It agreed to renew high-level relations with the European Union only after France caved in.

UNDERSTAND THE MULTIPLE LAYERS OF AUTHORITY

Given the size and magnitude of the country, the Chinese government faces many social problems, especially in the rural areas. The Chinese leadership looks favorably upon foreign companies that are genuinely interested in helping out with social issues, such as building schools for underprivileged children. But they have a complex approval system that sometimes involves the central government in Beijing (which ensures there is no political agenda in the sponsorship program). Once the program is approved at the very top, there is more work to be done to have it ready for implementation. The company's management must invest considerable time to find out who the people in the approval chain are—street authorities (such street leaders exist in very large cities), village heads, town councillors, city mayors, district secretaries (who could also be attached to the Party Secretary office), and mayors at the provincial level.

The positive side is that many of these city or district mayors welcome support for their respective social programs. They are also extremely helpful once the various levels of officials are on board for the program. For instance, Chinese officials in western Szechuan province were delighted to provide all the support to DreamWorks Animation studio for the production of *Kung Fu Panda 2*, which showcased the best of the scenic provincial capital—Chengdu. It all started with the 2008 Sichuan earthquake, after which officials at all levels were looking for external help. *Kung Fu Panda 2* has helped to put Chengdu on the global stage, and officials expect tourism to flourish with the new publicity. Drawn by the allure of Hollywood movies, more Chinese cities have started looking for similar tie-ups.

Despite the prevalence of corruption in China, more leaders at almost all levels are becoming increasingly aware that honesty and a bribe-free environment are essential for foreign multinational firms. In the same breath, it is equally important for foreign firms to establish a *modus operandi* of transparency and honesty. Once foreign firms have established this *modus operandi*, they will find it easier to be viewed as exemplary corporate citizens in China. Because CapitaLand made this social investment, it could very quickly play a role in supporting worthy causes when opportunities arose.

For instance, CapitaLand donated infrared fever scanners to China during the SARS epidemic in 2003 and was among the first corporations to pledge a donation of five million yuan for Sichuan earthquake relief in 2008. It sponsored cultural exchange programs between the two countries, such as sponsoring Chinese performances in Singapore and *vice versa*. CapitaLand has also collaborated with local authorities and charities in China to build CapitaLand Hope Schools and student dormitories (which are partially funded by the CapitaLand Hope Foundation). When building its first Hope School in Yunnan ten years ago, CapitaLand worked closely with the Shanghai authorities—China's overall Hope program was administered out of Beijing, and Beijing had made Shanghai responsible for all charitable work in the Yunnan area. It was serendipity that the Shanghai journalists showed a personal interest in this program and volunteered to join CapitaLand staff in pursing this charitable cause.

WEAK OVERSIGHT OF REGULATIONS

China does not lack regulations; what it lacks is oversight of these regulations. For example, it has over 200 laws regulating food safety standards at the national and regional levels. Yet, food-related problems are endemic. The classic case is the 2008 contaminated milk scandal, which affected nearly 300,000 children. Fearing unrest, the authorities initially detained parents of sickened children for several hours—to stop them from holding a press conference to complain about compensation arrangements. But public outrage and the extent of the scandal finally led to the death sentence for the boss and three other executives of Sanlu Group, the milk manufacturer.

Intellectual property rights is another problem area and one that is a source of growing friction between Beijing and the West (especially the United States). Gilheney razors, N-Mart Super Center, Future Cola, and Starsbuck are Chinese brands that echo some of the best-known US brands—Gillette, Walmart, Coca-Cola, and Starbucks. US businesses say that China's protection of intellectual property rights is ineffective and that piracy has damaged their operations in China. Frankfurt-listed Business Media China, which buys advertising concessions and had rights to run large exhibitions such as the China Beauty Expo in Shanghai, found that its senior Chinese managers had surreptitiously set up their own advertising and exhibition business within the company—the staff were siphoning off the most lucrative advertising contracts, which included billboard advertising at dozens of China's largest railway stations and airports.

In this flawed regulatory environment, there are opportunities for foreign firms to work with their Chinese business counterparts to bring international standards to the table. For example, CapitaLand worked closely with the relevant authorities to introduce sustainability and green features into its buildings across China. In 2008, it held a "Green Hope School Design" competition that involved top architectural students from China designing the CapitaLand Muchuan Green Hope School in Sichuan province. The winning design was built and completed in 2009; this was followed by a campaign to recruit volunteer teachers for the school. Over 10,000 interested applicants signed up for the 26 places available—a testimony to the success of CapitaLand's outreach efforts. In 2010, CapitaLand was conferred the "China Best Corporate Citizen" award for the third year running by the China Committee of Corporate Citizenship and CCTV2. Such public and government recognition goes a long way toward building good relations with the various government ministries and agencies.

SOFT POWER AND BRAND EQUITY

The rise of China as a global power coincides with the decline of the United States as a superpower and the economic woes of Western Europe and Japan. A decade ago, China was not the top trading partner for even one of the Group of 20 economies. Today, it is the biggest trading partner for six (Australia, India, Japan, Korea, Russia, and South Africa), and it has displaced the United States as the top export market for the seventh (Brazil). China is also a major importer for these countries. Therefore, there is a need for a measure of deference to the Chinese way of doing business.

This includes understanding that China likes big events that bring the country onto the world stage and that emphasize its role as the Middle Kingdom. The Chinese make much of symbols and anniversary dates. For example, the nation had its Olympic moment at 8.08 PM on the eighth day of the eighth month of the eighth year of China's eighth millennium as a civilization.

After the turn of the 20th century, the Chinese government organized a multiyear series of high-profile international events—the Beijing Olympics in 2008, the Shanghai Expo in 2010, and the Guangzhou Asian Games in 2010. These major events have one thing in common—they convey the message that China can take international events to new heights of razzmatazz. They help project the Party leadership's credentials and tell the people how the country has developed into an international player. "A new Beijing, a new Olympics" was one of China's slogans for the Olympics.

However, to manage its global brand equity, China will have to change its communication style. It will need to review and rewrite its communication strategies to contend with critics in the West and be sensitive to regional diplomatic issues. For example, the country has been aggressively asserting its maritime territorial claims in the South China Sea. Historically, it has advocated and exported communism to these Asian countries while not having compromised on maritime claims. It seized the Paracel Islands from Vietnam in 1974, was involved in a bloody clash with Vietnam near Johnson Reef in 1988, and bullied the Philippines over the possession of Mischief Reef in 1994 and 1999. In its pursuit of capitalist growth, it suspended this aggressive political stance for about a decade. In recent years, however, it has reverted to type and acted stridently and uncompromisingly on issues related to territorial integrity.

China's leadership is aware that its aggressive political and military stance on regional issues will affect the reputation of Chinese companies with an international footprint. China is the biggest direct investor in South America. In Brazil, for example, it has deals in mining, steel, construction equipment, and electricity transmission. It is also making investments in infrastructure and industry in Africa, the Middle East, Central Asia, and South Asia. Indeed, China's growth is felt in nearly every corner of the globe. Because of its aggressive ways, it is not always welcome. The classic example of foreign governments rejecting Chinese companies is when China National Offshore Oil Corporation—the listed arm of China's largest offshore petroleum giant—announced plans in 2005 to acquire Unocal, a US oil firm. Its attempts to acquire the company were blocked by the US government.

Nonetheless, China has started to invest in its global communication. Its recent initiatives include the setting up of a public diplomacy research center; producing an international image-building film; and setting up Confucius Institutes worldwide. Chinese rail companies are bidding for and building high-speed rail projects in the United States, Australia, Argentina, Thailand, Kazakhstan, and many other countries. Who can say no to a little high-speed diplomacy?

When the Bush administration was waging wars in Iraq and Afghanistan, US companies banded together to form Business for Diplomatic Action (BDA) to protect the interests of US brands. International firms operating in China can help Chinese companies create a BDA equivalent—such an initiative can help China's globally focused companies to professionalize their global brand.

With more Chinese cities looking for tie-ups after DreamWorks Animation studio's *Kung Fu Panda 2,* US companies could ride on the allure of Hollywood movies and benefit from this ultimate soft power vehicle.

MAINSTREAM MEDIA IS STILL TIGHTLY CONTROLLED

The media scene in China has changed dramatically. When Deng Xiaoping made his famous declaration about opening up China to economic growth, only about ten million Chinese households had television sets. Today, programs such as China Central Television's Lunar New Year show attract more than 500 million Chinese viewers watching on 350 million television sets. The television sector is expected to generate over US$10 billion in advertising revenues in 2012. China will become the world's third-largest advertising economy, behind the United States and Japan. China's giant media conglomerates are capable of competing in the global marketplace.

Media is big business in China. When China said it would allow foreign companies more leeway to invest in the country's media, many big as well as small publishers, international TV companies, film studios, and newspaper executives were excited by the prospect of big profits. International media corporations—Bertelsmann of Germany, Viacom and Time Warner of the United States, and Phoenix TV of Hong Kong—announced plans to work with local operators. However, China's media regulators back-pedaled on the original plan and restricted foreign investors to one joint venture each.

Regulations take precedence over commercial imperatives, so running a media business in China is not like running a media business anywhere else in the world. China's media conglomerates cannot neglect their propaganda role. In fact, there is Party oversight of their business operations. For instance, the Beijing

Radio, Film and Television Group is scrutinized by the Beijing Publicity Department under the Administration of Radio, Film and Television (Sarft).

While the Chinese government may want the economic benefits of opening up its markets to foreigners, it still wants to have a tight grip over the media. Chinese paramilitary police continue to detain and question reporters if they touch on sensitive issues. Mainstream media must carry the official line, especially Party leaders' warnings on sensitive subjects such as political dissidents.

China's media coverage of domestic and international events has portrayed conflicting images of the country: it is supremely proud and confident on the one hand, yet suffers from massive insecurity (bordering on paranoia) on the other.

SOCIAL MEDIA HAS GREAT IMPACT IN CHINA

The Internet has overtaken the mainstream media as a communication platform for vigorous public debate, which hardly existed in China a decade ago. In the past, news of dissent was seldom available to foreign journalists. But today, with the Internet and mobile telephony, these protests come to light regularly. So, while Chinese officials often try to cover up disturbances to avoid trouble with their superiors, they have sometimes been forced by citizens' Internet postings to meet the protestors and address their grievances.

However, censorship of the Internet has increased. The networking site LinkedIn was blocked after it was used to spread calls for a Jasmine-style revolution in 2011. Sites such as Twitter and Facebook—which were integral to the democracy movements in the Middle East—have long been blocked in China.

The authorities try to block sensitive discussions on "microblogs" using keyword filters and an army of "Net nannies." But the impact of these efforts is limited, as savvy users quickly find ways of circumventing government blocks. One clever technique has been to use online software to render Chinese-language script vertically instead of horizontally.

Against this seemingly negative backdrop, what can companies do to ensure positive traction for themselves in China? CapitaLand, for example, decided to embrace social media to build its corporate brand. Using feedback from Nielsen and other survey reports, CapitaLand identified the core online publications in China and managed them as part of the group's media management strategies. For example, it invited representatives from these online publications to participate in a tour of its Singapore operations as well as its Australian properties.

In another initiative, CapitaLand created an online game that tapped into Netizens' desire to seek information, have fun, win prizes, and socialize with others. Gamers could translate the points they won into vouchers that could be used at various malls or at Ascott serviced apartments in China. Between March 2010 and June 2010, the game attracted about 800,000 visitors and over 3.2 million page views.

However, having a "totem pole" brand position in China also attracts spammers, domain name thefts, and other similar disquietudes. For example, there are online publishers who will first post negative stories about a company and then blackmail the company into coughing up "advertising support" (in return for "rectifying" the negative stories). Hence, companies would do well to be vigilant of social media shenanigans.

CONCLUSION

In conclusion, laying the groundwork to keep abreast of developments in China is critical to the Corporate Affairs function. In China, Corporate Affairs is still in its early stages, even among multinational companies; it is even more in the infancy stage for Chinese companies. Herein lie great opportunities.

◆ KEY TAKEAWAYS ◆

- Consider major events and hold parallel events that dovetail with your business.
- At major events, be mindful of potential downsides generated by Western NGOs, etc. Expect government intervention to quell dissent.
- Plan for charitable and cause–related projects. Work closely with the multiple layers of government ministries and agencies.
- China does not lack regulations, but it lacks unified supervision and control. This provides opportunities for lobbying/public affairs activities.
- Where appropriate, manage Corporate Affairs to support China's soft power strategies.
- The media is watched carefully by the Chinese government.
- The Internet/social media is a powerful medium. Have an active online strategy without upsetting the authorities.

References

A waking dragon shakes the world. *Financial Times*, 30 December 2004.

Anderlini, J. A cautionary tale from China. *Financial Times*, 27 July 2009.

Banyan: may the good China preserve us. *The Economist*. 21 May 2009.

Barboza, D. For Chinese brands, an effort to "go global." *The New York Times*, 29 June 2005.

Baum, R. (2010). *China Watcher: Confessions of a Peking Tom*. Seattle: University of Washington Press.

Berkofsky, A. China's Asian ambitions. *Far Eastern Economic Review*, July/August 2005.

China and the Internet, again. Review and outlook [Editorial]. *The Asian Wall Street Journal*, 27 September 2005.

China looks at revamp of state media groups. *The Business Times* [Singapore], 19 April 2005.

China seeks to reassure on "peaceful development." *International Herald Tribune*, 25 April 2005.

China's schizophrenic faces. Recent events highlight the paradox of a confident, rising power that is yet fragile and insecure. *Today* [Singapore], 5 March 2011.

Chinese business: time to change the act. *The Economist*, 19 February 2009.

Ching, C. Why Beijing can't let Xinjiang fester. *The Straits Times* [Singapore], 24 July 2009.

Ching, F. The bottom line: don't let China lose its soul in drive to modernize. *The Business Times* [Singapore], 30 March 2005.

Chua, J. Media, a minefield, rather than a goldmine. Foreign companies seeking to invest in the media industry will have to live with Beijing keeping a tight rein on them. *The Business Times* [Singapore], 20 April 2005.

Coming out: China hopes to use the 2008 Olympics in Beijing to mark its emergence on the world stage. *The Economist, 23 March 2006.*

Dyer, G. World economy: the China cycle. *Financial Times*, 12 September 2010.

Dyer, G. Nervous China puts security apparatus into overdrive. *Financial Times*, 23 February 2011.

Dyer, G., Hille, K. and Waldmeir, P. Chinese steer clear of "Jasmine Revolution." *Financial Times*, 20 February 2011.

French, H.W. Chinese pushing back against Net censorship. *The New York Times*, 5 February 2008.

Johnson, I. China blocks Internet over protest calls. *International Herald Tribune*, 26 February 2011.

Kahn, J. China gives Zhao's death scant notice. *The New York Times*, 18 January 2005.

Kang, B.L. and Kitano, M. China, Japan mend fences, but pitfalls ahead. *Reuters News Agency*, 24 April 2005.

Kynge, J., McGregor, R., Dombey, D., Arnold, M., Warrell, H. and O'Murchu, C. The China syndrome. *Financial Times*, 3 March 2011.

Lafraniere, S. A rattled China keeps watch over foreigners; journalists are restricted and events vetoed; some cellphones to be tracked. *International Herald Tribune*, 4 March 2011.

Liew, M.L. Towards Asian renaissance: the rise of China—a business perspective. *The Business Times* [Singapore], 31 October 2009.

Lim, M.Y. Riding on the dragon's tailwind. *The Business Times* [Singapore], 11 July 2011.

McGregor, R. and Gluck, C. China to foil Taiwan independence "at any cost." *Financial Times*, 27 December 2004.

Opinion lessons from China and India: the rise of China and India will shift world's centre of gravity from the Atlantic to the Pacific and Indian Oceans. *The Business Times* [Singapore], 5 April 2005.

O'Neill, M. Technology: China's long march to globalisation. *South China Morning Post* [Hong Kong], 7 February 2005.

Peh, S.H. New ways needed to manage society, CCP told. *The Straits Times* [Singapore], 24 February 2011.

Pilling, D. Could China's rulers be right to be jittery? *Financial Times*, 24 February 2011.

Protests in China—the cauldron boils. *The Economist*, 29 September 2005.

Siow, M. Image makeover could do with more finesse. *Today* [Singapore], 22 October 2010.

The new world order: how China sees the world, and how the world should see China. *The Economist*, 19 March 2009.

Torch goes to Tibet and Xinjiang: security stepped up and people told to stay home as Olympic flame stops at restive regions. *The Straits Times* [Singapore], 17 June 2007.

Tse, E. (2010). *The China Strategy: Harnessing the Power of the World's Fastest-growing Economy*. New York: Basic Books.

Wasserstrom, J.N. (2010). *China in the 21st Century: What Everyone Needs to Know*. New York: Oxford University Press.

Whyte, M.K. (2010). *Myth of the Social Volcano: Perceptions of Inequality and Distributive Injustice in Contemporary China*. Stanford, CA: Stanford University Press.

Wilson, E. Slums for the masses, fortunes for the few. *The Spectator*, 3 November 2007.

Winchester, S. (2008). *Bomb, Book and Compass: Joseph Needham and the Great Secrets of China*. London: Penguin Books/Viking.

Winchester, S. (2008). *The Man Who Loved China: The Fantastic Story of the Eccentric Scientist Who Unlocked the Mysteries of the Middle Kingdom*. New York: HarperCollins.

Yeh, A. China's copycats dig their claws in: from lighters to Peking duck, nothing is safe. *Financial Times*, 2 February 2005.

Yeh, A. and Sanchanta, M. Japan calls for apology from China over riots. *Financial Times*, 10 April 2005.

INDEX